HAMILTON
A PEOPLE'S HISTORY

BILL FREEMAN
CONTEMPORARY PHOTOGRAPHY BY SIMON WILSON

JAMES LORIMER & COMPANY LTD., PUBLISHERS
TORONTO

James Lorimer & Company Ltd. acknowledges the support of the Ontario Arts Council. We acknowledge the support of the Government of Canada through the Book Publishing Industry Development Program (BPIDP) for our publishing activities. We acknowledge the support of the Canada Council for the Arts for our publishing program.

Canadian Cataloguing in Publication Data

Freeman, Bill, 1938–
    Hamilton: a people's history
    Includes index.
    ISBN 10: 1-55028-936-5 ISBN 13: 978-1-55028-936-7
1. Hamilton (Ont.) – History. I. Title.
FC3098.4.F74 2001   971.3'5204   C2001-901223-3
F1059.5.H2F74 2001

James Lorimer & Company Ltd., Publishers
317 Atlantic Street West, Suite #1002
Toronto, Ontario
M5V 1P9
www.lorimer.ca

Printed and bound in Canada.

For the people of Hamilton,
past and present.

CONTENTS

FOREWORD

Hamiltonians take great pride in the people, places, and events that have shaped our history and defined our community. Bill Freeman's book, *Hamilton: A People's History*, reinforces that pride. This book colourfully celebrates our past and the many accomplishments of the remarkable people of Hamilton.

Aboriginal hunters paddled their canoes along the lake in the distant past. Etienne Brule explored the shoreline in 1616. The first settlers came in 1776. George Hamilton laid out the future of our community 1813.

Between the covers of this book, the stories of many of those who chose Hamilton as their home come alive: Robert Land, a United Empire Loyalist and refugee from the American War of Independence; penniless Irish who fled the ravages of famine in the 1840s; and the thousands of newcomers from every corner of the world who came to our shores after the Second World War in search of peace and prosperity. They came from the United Kingdom, the United States, Italy, and Poland. There were also refugees from central Europe and the Baltic States. They, in turn, were followed by the huge post-war influx of the Dutch and Germans and by yet more waves of Polish and Italian immigrants. They, too, were followed by Hungarians, Portuguese, South Asians, and West Indians. Each

generation sought to build a better life, a vibrant community, and a stronger country.

Throughout Hamilton are the physical reminders of the endurance and bravery and wisdom and toil of those who came before us—Dundurn Castle, the Armoury, Whitehern, Hamilton Waterworks, Hamilton Customs House, the Battlefield Monument. Each is a place where we can walk in the steps of previous generations and sense the connection with Hamiltonians over the ages.

Hamilton's achievements go beyond bricks and mortar. Hamiltonians led the drive for public education, and we continue that tradition with one of the finest universities and community colleges, as well as public school systems, in the province. Free medical and birth control clinics were built early in the twentieth century. And it was here that industrial unionism was firmly established in Canada during the 1946 strikes.

The contrasts of Hamilton are often striking. Steel factories perch alongside one end of the harbour, while at the other end are Cootes Paradise, the Royal Botanical Gardens, and the future home of the Canada Discovery Centre.

Hamilton is a sporting town of keen rivalries, but we are also a community that rallied together to build Hamilton Place and the

Canadian Football Hall of Fame. Hamilton is a city committed to becoming a model of sustainable development for the twenty-first century, but one that still comes together on Saturday mornings at the Farmers' Market, just as Hamiltonians have been doing since 1837.

Hamilton is proud of its labour history and equally proud that it has the highest number of people with doctorates, per capita, in Canada. It is an industrial city, but with the highest per capita amount of green space of any city in the country.

Hamilton's spirit is perhaps best illustrated in the story of Billy Sherring, a modest railway porter from a North End family, who became a world-class runner. In 1906, Billy travelled at his own expense to Athens, Greece to face the world's best marathon runners in the first Olympics of the modern era. With the grit and determination of a true Hamiltonian, he won that race and set a world record.

Read *Hamilton: A People's History* and hear the voices of the men and women who came before us—listen to their dreams, marvel at their discipline, sympathize with their fears, share their enthusiasms, learn about their families, and come to know them as the builders of Hamilton.

My congratulations to Bill Freeman and to all of those who have laboured so hard and with so much passion to put together this book. May they inspire all of us to be stewards of our heritage.

— The Honourable Sheila Copps

PREFACE

Hamilton has long been a fascination of mine. I remember as a child driving down the escarpment at night. My father would point excitedly and say: "Look! The magic city!" To my young eyes the lights twinkling below us were truly magical. When I moved to Hamilton as a young man, I came to love the physical features of the region: the Niagara Escarpment, the bay, and the Dundas Valley. But the real joy for me was the people I met in the city.

Hamilton: A People's History is the result of that fascination with the city and its people. It is a work of popular history. In these pages you will not find the debates of academic historians; rather, my focus is on the story of the city and the people who have lived here. Any story is shaped by the interests of its writer. I make no apologies for this. All I can hope is that my interests reflect those of my readers and that the descriptions accurately capture the events that were important in the development of the city.

This book is the companion piece to the television program broadcast by CH-TV called *Hamilton: Where the Rubber Meets the Road.* I had decided to write a popular history of the city, and David Wesley, of Red Canoe Productions, took the idea of a film based on the research to CH-TV. The station's enthusiastic commitment to broadcasting the program and its financial support made the project possible. John Morrow, of Whitewater Media, shot and directed the film and a co-wrote the film project with me.

There are many people to thank in the creation of this book. David Wesley has been a good sounding board for my ideas. Rachel Zolf and Pam Tyrell collected many of the images, and Jane

Mountain played an essential administrative role. Brian Henley and Margaret Houghton of Special Collections at the Hamilton Public Library were also of great assistance. Margaret deserves special mention for her stellar efforts in collecting visuals for the book.

As part of the film project, David Wesley assembled people interested in Hamilton history to serve as a resource group for the project. Most of these folks were active in the Head of the Lake Historical Society. Others were connected with the Ontario Workers' Arts and Heritage Centre and McMaster University. The discussions of that group brought many new issues and insights to me. I only hope that the film and this book are adequate reward for their hours of participation. The members of the group were: Right Honourable Lincoln Alexander, Melville Bailey, Nancy Bouchier, Bob Bratina, Roxy Browne, Nina Chapple, Walter Cooke, Ken Cruikshank, David Cuming, Frank DeNardis, James Elliot, Jeff Feswick, Robert Fraser, Carolyn Gray, Gary Hall, Marilynn Havelka, Renee Johnston, Stewart Leslie, Wayne Lewchuk, Dennis Missett, Richard Moll, Jane Mulkewich, Walter Peace, Michael Quigley, Kathy Renwald, Lori Rosenberg, John Weaver, and John Wigle.

Finally, I would like to give special thanks to the many journalists and writers who have written about Hamilton over the years. This book would never have been possible without their insights. The debt I own them is reflected in my liberal use of their words on the pages that follow.

Bill Freeman

Chapter One

THE HEAD OF THE LAKE
(From Beginnings to 1814)

E ons ago, in a warm tropical sea, the limestone ridge we call the Niagara Escarpment was formed. Slowly, the land rose above sea level. Glaciers advanced and retreated, the last as recently as 12,000 years ago. Soon, the land was covered with dense forests, streams, and lakes as clear as glass.

The Neutrals

About 6,000 years ago, human habitation began at the Head of the Lake, the western end of Lake Ontario. For centuries, Native people fished along the shores of the lake and the bay, hunted for game in the forests, and grew corn and squash in the fertile soil. This was the centre of the territory of a people the French called the Neutrals because they remained neutral between the two dominant groups in the region: the Iroquois, who lived south of Lake Ontario, and the Hurons, who lived along Georgian Bay.

We do not know a lot about the Neutrals,

but it is believed that they numbered about 40,000 before the Europeans arrived. Their territory included the Niagara Peninsula and crossed the Niagara River into western New York State. French traders and missionaries visited them early in the seventeenth century and found that they had a culture similar to other peoples' in the

An early view of Cootes Paradise.

Aboriginal peoples and European traders used freight canoes such as this to transport their furs and trade goods on Lake Ontario.

probably near what we call La Salle Park. A group of them climbed up the mountain, where their leader was frightened by a rattlesnake, and then they pushed further west into the wilderness by canoe.

By 1700, this area was firmly established as French territory. A fur trading post, called Toronto, was built at the mouth of the Humber River, and a larger fort and trading post was established at the mouth of the Niagara River. Where Spenser Creek emptied into Coote's Paradise, at a place we call the Town of Dundas, there was a storage depot where the

Eastern Woodlands. They lived in fortified villages beside lakes and streams. The women looked after the planting and harvesting of the crops while the men hunted and fished. The Neutrals controlled the quarrying of flint and slate near the present town of Fort Erie, and there is evidence of extensive trading of these and other items among all of the people in eastern North America.

But the coming of the Europeans brought disaster to the Neutrals. Their numbers were diminished by the smallpox epidemic of 1638–40, and though they tried to stay out of the war that engulfed the Native people of the area it did them little good. In 1650, the Iroquois attacked their enemies, the Hurons, killing or scattering the members of this powerful nation. Then they turned on the Neutrals. Almost nothing is known about that war, but legend has it that the last stand of the Neutrals was at Burlington Heights, a place we now call Dundurn Park. All we can know for certain is that 40,000 people disappeared and the Neutral Nation vanished.

In 1669, when Robert René Cavelier de La Salle and his party of French explorers came into the bay on an expedition that took them down the Mississippi to the Gulf of Mexico, there was no trace of the Neutrals. The party stayed for a few days, camping on the north shore,

traders kept their furs and trade goods. The Native people who had moved into the area occupying the lands of the Neutrals were Mississaugas of the Ojibwa Nation.

The growing competition between the French and the English in the eighteenth century for the domination of North America gradually came to a climax in the 1750s. After a series of early French victories in the Seven Years War, the strength of English numbers and the power of the British navy began to take their toll. A group led by Sir William Johnson captured Fort Niagara and the French were forced to abandon Lake Ontario. With the English victory in 1759 at the Battle of the Plains of Abraham, the French domination of the region came to an end.

Tshusick, an Ojibwa woman

The Loyalists

But the determining struggle that established the settlement patterns for this region was not the French and English war; it was the American War of Independence. When that war broke out in 1775, it pitted the Rebels, or Patriots as they are now called, against the British. A substantial number of people who lived in what is now the United States remained loyal to the British crown. As the war drew to a close in 1783, and it became clear that the British had lost, many of those people chose to leave their homes rather than live under American rule.

In all, about 60,000 Loyalists came north to live in the colonies that today make up Canada. Most went to Nova Scotia and New Brunswick, but approximately 10,000 came to Upper Canada. Of that group, about 2,000 came to the Niagara Peninsula, including the area known at the time as the Head of the Lake. This is how one person described the hardships of the Loyalists who travelled overland to this part of the country:

An artistic portrayal of the Loyalists drawing lots for their farmland.

On foot, on horseback and by homemade boat portaged laboriously from stream to stream, by oxcart and by Conestoga [wagon]…through the dense unfriendly wilderness, strife-worn, hungry, and frequently destitute men, women and children followed the trails north. Reaching the Niagara River, refugees crossed the stream on rudely constructed rafts, or dismantling their wagons and caulking the seams with clay, paddled their household goods across while they swam their farm animals alongside.

—Marjorie Freeman Campbell[1]

There are many stories of the hardships of the Loyalists and how they came to shape the settlement of this region. The following are just four.

Joseph Brant and the Iroquois Loyalists

At the outbreak of the American Revolutionary War, the Iroquois Confederacy of the Six Nations lived in their traditional territory in northern New York State. At the urging of Joseph Brant, a Mohawk war chief, and others, the confederacy joined with their British allies against the American rebels.

The Iroquois, and the Mohawks in particular, were among the most effective units of the British forces. Joseph Brant was commissioned as an officer but fought as a war chief. The Iroquois harassed the rebels in several engagements, spreading terror among American settlers. Brant and his Mohawk warriors were involved in the Cherry Valley raid in which a number of settlers were killed and accusations were made that innocent people had been slaughtered. In response, George Washington ordered a campaign to punish the Iroquois. An American invading force entered their territory, burning villages, destroying orchards, and spreading their own terror.

As the war drew to a close, it became clear that the British were going to lose. Brant and others appealed to

Thayendanegea, or Joseph Brant, as he looked when he lived in Wellington Square (Burlington).

the British, and Governor Haldimand granted them lands including a large tract along the Grand River. In May of 1784, Brant led the Mohawk and other Iroquois Loyalists into Canada, to their new home at what is now called the Six Nations Reserve near Cayuga.

Joseph Brant actively worked for the British cause to the end of his life. After the war, he attempted to form a united confederation of the Iroquois and Native people in the west in order to block American expansion, but this ultimately failed. He was given 1,000 acres of land in Burlington, just north of the Beach Strip, where he established a farm and built a magnificent house overlooking the bay and Lake Ontario. There, he lived almost like an English gentleman, with servants to run his household and farm. His house still stands and is used today as a museum.

Controversy followed Brant for the rest of his life. Tragically, he killed his own son after a violent argument. He was also involved in the scheme to sell Iroquois land along the Grand River. The plan was to invest the profits from the sale of this land for future generations, but there was a surplus of land in those days and the project was not well managed. In the end, the Iroquois lost a great deal of their original land grant and gained little in return. But Brant remained revered by his people, and when he died in 1807 he was honoured by all of the people in Upper Canada.

Robert Land[2]

In 1775, Robert Land was a prosperous farmer who lived with his wife Phoebe and seven children in New York State, on the banks of the Delaware River. When war broke out he chose the Loyalist side and volunteered for the British army. Land was not attached to a regular unit but gathered information and carried dispatches through rebel held territory.

While he was away, the Patriots targeted the Land family. His oldest son John was thrown in prison. One night, 16-year-old Kate was awakened by a Native telling her to go to another Loyalist family who lived across the river. There, she found that all the members of this family had been killed and their house burned. Returning home, the Native warned her that they were about to be attacked. Kate woke her mother and the rest of the family and they fled into a cornfield where they hid while their home was torched and burned to the ground. When daylight came, the family fled, and with the help of friends finally found shelter in New York City, a British stronghold.

Not long after this, Robert Land found time for a stealthy visit to his family. Finding the charred remains of his house and knowing the hatred of his neighbours, he assumed that his family had all been killed. Heartsick, he decided to leave and never return. He arranged to have a Quaker friend named Morden lead him to Niagara, but they were pursued by the rebels. Land fled, he was shot at, and one of the bullets struck his backpack, knocking him to the ground. As he fell, he cut his hand and, bleeding profusely, escaped as fast as he could manage. The rebels, seeing the blood and believing that he was dead, turned on Morden. Although the Quaker's religious beliefs forbade him from engaging in the war, he was hanged on the spot.

Robert Land managed to make his way to the Niagara frontier. In time, he was granted 200 acres of land within hearing distance of Niagara Falls, where he stayed for two years. But Land was heartsick and depressed. He decided to move as far away from the border as he could and struck inland towards the Head of the Lake. Finally, he squatted on a piece of property within what is today the City of Hamilton and built a lean-to at about the intersection of present-day Barton and Leeming Streets. There, he farmed a little and lived off the land, hunting and fishing.

Meanwhile, at the end of the war, Phoebe Land and the other members of the family went with Loyalist refugees to New Brunswick. They remained there for seven years, but things did not go well for the family. Robert, the youngest son, was dissatisfied and urged his mother to move to Upper Canada where he had heard that conditions were better. Phoebe eventually agreed. They travelled by way of New York and visited their farm by the Delaware, which the oldest son John had taken over. John urged them to stay, but they were

Settlers often planted their crops between the stumps on their newly-cleared land.

determined to live under the British flag. Finally, they crossed the Niagara River and settled near the falls.

Two years later, one of the brothers heard from a trader that there was a man by the name of Land who lived near the Head of the Lake. Phoebe had always held a faint hope that her husband might still be alive, and when they heard this the family set off on the 40-mile trek. The story that has come down to us is that Robert Land was sitting in front of his lean-to, smoking his pipe, and contemplating his sad fate, when his family broke into the clearing. The reunion must have been an overwhelmingly emotional moment for all of them.

Restored by the reunion, the Land family grew and prospered. They came to own 1,000 acres, encompassing several farms, stretching from the mountain to the bay and from Wellington Street to east of Emerald. To commemorate the happy reunion, Robert Land planted a weeping willow tree that flourished for many years.

Richard Beasley[3]

"The first settler at the Head of the Lake," is the inscription on the headstone of Richard Beasley. There is some dispute about this statement. Robert Land and Richard Beasley both settled in what is

A view of the Coote's Paradise shoreline as early settlers would have found it, by Henry McEvoy.

Lady Simcoe's 1796 sketch looking west from Burlington Heights towards Coote's Paradise.

now Hamilton in the year 1786. Some believe that Charles Depew, who took land around Sherman and Burlington Streets, preceded both of them, but Richard Beasley came to the area when the Head of the Lake was wilderness.

Beasley grew up in the Albany, New York area and at the age of 16 joined the Loyalist cause. He was captured by the Rebels but managed to get free, and made his way to Niagara by 1777 to become one of the first of the Loyalist refugees. There, he was employed as a storekeeper by the British Army and established good relations with the Iroquois that benefitted him all of his life. Soon, Beasley became an independent trader, operating from Toronto to Niagara and the Head of the Lake. Sometime around 1786, he acquired 200 acres of land near Paradise Road and Main Street West, where he built a crude log house. From this location he carried on his trading and business activities.

One day, while he was out riding along the shore of Coote's Paradise, Beasley came across a distraught young Loyalist woman. This was Hannah Springer. She had been captured by Seneca warriors and was to be given for adoption to a Seneca mother who had lost her own children. Hannah had managed to escape, but had become hopelessly lost. When Beasley found her, she was terrified that she might be recaptured. Beasley returned Hannah to her own family, and later the couple was married and had seven children. One of them, Henry, born in 1793, was the first child of European origin born at the Head of the Lake.

Richard Beasley prospered from trading and land speculation. Sometime in the early 1790s, he built himself a fine house on Burlington Heights, on the spot where Dundurn Castle is today. By this time, he was one of the most important people at the Head of the Lake, and much more prosperous than most of the Loyalist refugees who were struggling to establish themselves in this inhospitable environment. In 1791, he was elected to the legislature and later became the Justice of the Peace and Magistrate.

A life long Tory, Beasley played a prominent role in the colony for many years. He is best remembered for his confusing business dealings around the sale of the Iroquois lands in Waterloo County. Because of his friendship with Joseph Brant, Beasley acquired the right to sell Block II of this land, consisting of 94,012 acres. Mennonites from Pennsylvania settled here, but later found that Beasley had not discharged a mortgage that he had put against the property. There were accusations of fraud, and Beasley narrowly avoided debtors' prison or criminal charges. What ultimately saved him was that the Mennonites found the land to their satisfaction and raised enough money to pay off the obligation.

Despite the cloud that hung over his business dealings, good fortune seemed to stay with Beasley the rest of his life. In 1803, he was made Speaker of the Legislative Assembly and in 1804 was appointed to the Legislative Council. He remained active in politics and business until after the War of 1812 and lived until 1842, by which time Hamilton had become a thriving centre. His son and grandson were prominent in the affairs of the city into the twentieth century.

Mary Gage[4]

In 1790, Mary Gage and her two children, sixteen-year-old James and fourteen-year-old Elizabeth, loaded what few possessions they could carry into a canoe and left their home on the Hudson River near Albany. It had been a difficult time for the family. Mary's husband, John Gage, had been a Loyalist officer in the British Army and had been killed in the American Revolutionary War. The family suffered at the hands of their neighbours and felt that they had to abandon their home.

Travelling up the Mohawk River, they crossed the portage to Wood Creek and then paddled down the Oswego River to Lake

Settlers often gathered for big projects such as barn raisings.

prominent Loyalists. Soon after their arrival, the Gage family was granted 200 acres of land in Saltfleet Township and took up farming.

Life was not easy. Mary Gage cleared the land and tilled the soil with her two children until James was old enough to take over the responsibility. Elizabeth married and moved to Brant County. James married Mary Davis from a Loyalist family that had settled at Albion Falls and together they had nine children. James turned the Gage home at Stoney Creek into a store, the first store in the area and one of the principal stopping places between Niagara and York (Toronto). Later, he was involved in a number of businesses. Mary Gage lived until 1841 and died at the age of 97.

Settlement

Once the Loyalists crossed the Niagara River they were welcomed by the British administrators, but their problems were far from over. Most who came to Ontario were farmers. Many had lived on the frontier and were experienced woodsmen. These were people who knew how to look after themselves in the wilderness, but even they found it a struggle to make a living in this remote and isolated part of Canada.

When they first arrived, the families had to camp for several days while surveyors set the lot lines. Former army officers were given preference and usually got the best land, along the waterfront. Most families were given 200 acres and were supplied with clothes for three years, blankets, and some rudimentary tools. Squatters' rights were also recognized in cases where settlers moved onto land before it was surveyed.

Ontario. Following the shore of the lake, they headed west in their small canoe until they arrived at Newark (present-day Niagara-on-the-Lake). Though they were now safely in British territory, the Gage family headed out again, following the shore of Lake Ontario until they arrived at Stoney Creek.

Mary Gage's brother, Augustus Jones, had settled in Stoney Creek. Augustus was a surveyor who laid out a number of the townships and roads in Upper Canada. He had married a daughter of a Mississauga chief and was friendly with Joseph Brant and other

The area on top of the mountain was easier to settle because the forest was not as dense. Below the mountain the soil was richer, but streams created bogs and marshes. Immense trees and thick underbrush were everywhere. Inlets from the bay made travel difficult. A road ran under the mountain from Newark to the Head of the Lake, but it was little more than a path that was impassable for wagons in the early years. Most people travelled by boat or canoe whenever possible.

Families would clear a little land and build a shelter of sorts, usually a rough log lean-to. At first, the settlers planted their crops between the tree stumps. The years 1787 and 1788 were called "the Hungry Years." Drought came and all the crops failed, but game was plentiful. Deer were hunted for meat and their hides were used for clothing. Fish abounded in streams, the bay, and the lake. Rabbits, bears, squirrels, and porcupine were plentiful, as well as duck, geese, wild turkey, and passenger pigeons. Berries, wild mushrooms, and root crops grew, and many learned how to tap the maple trees and boil down the sap into maple syrup. Everyone had a smokehouse for curing fish and meat, and root cellars kept vegetables from freezing in winter and kept them cool in summer.

Many settlers traveled to Upper Canada by ox-cart, bringing all their worldly possessions with them.

But there were dangers. Rattlesnakes abounded, and domestic animals had to be watched constantly. Pigs could forage for themselves, but they became wild. When farmers went out to get their hogs, they carried guns in case they were attacked by their own animals. This is a recollection of John Ryckman, who was born in 1798:

The city was then all forest through which roamed bears and wolves. The shores of the bay were difficult to reach or to see because they were hidden by a thick, almost impenetrable mass of trees and undergrowth. There were no roads. There was only one cow-path to Niagara and one to Caledonia. People could travel readily on water in canoes or bateaux, but on land they traveled on foot or on horseback… Bears ate pigs so the settlers warred on bears. Wolves gobbled up sheep and geese so they had to hunt and trap the wolves. They also held organized raids on rattlesnakes on the mountainside. There was plenty of game. Many a time I have seen a deer jump over the fence into my backyard and there were millions of pigeons[5], which we killed with clubs as they flew low. I saw 112 killed with one shot.

—John Ryckman[6]

In those days, money was almost unknown, and a type of barter system developed. Groceries were paid for in grain. In 1794, 100 acres of land bounded by Main Street in the south, Barton in the north, Emerald in the east, and Victoria in the west was sold for a barrel of pork and a yoke of oxen. Itinerant peddlers from the United States visited the remote settlements and sold their wares from wagons and carts.

Settlers relied on their neighbours. There were house- and barn-raising bees where everyone gathered to construct big projects. The bees usually finished with a party and dance. Neighbours were relied on at harvest time, especially if there was trouble such as sickness or injuries. Women often worked together to wash wool and to spin and weave it into cloth.

Religion was important. Many of the Loyalists were members of the Church of England (Anglican) but the Methodists in rural areas grew in number and influence. Meeting Houses built as places where the community could gather were also used as churches. The first in the area was in Stoney Creek, and another was built in Ancaster. Methodist circuit riders visited their scattered congregations on horseback and often conducted services in barns and houses.

An artist's depiction of the first meeting of the Legislature of Upper Canada.

The Simcoes

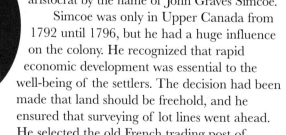

Governor John Graves Simcoe.

In May 1791, the British Parliament passed the Constitutional Act, dividing the colony into Upper and Lower Canada. It provided for a Legislative Assembly of sixteen representatives elected by the people and appointed a Legislative Council of seven councillors and a Lieutenant-Governor. The first Governor of Upper Canada was an English aristocrat by the name of John Graves Simcoe.

Simcoe was only in Upper Canada from 1792 until 1796, but he had a huge influence on the colony. He recognized that rapid economic development was essential to the well-being of the settlers. The decision had been made that land should be freehold, and he ensured that surveying of lot lines went ahead. He selected the old French trading post of Toronto as the capital, renaming it York, and ordered two important roads to be surveyed, Yonge Street and Dundas Street, which stimulated settlement. The governor used his influence to make slavery illegal in the colony and encouraged American settlers in the belief that they would soon adopt tory values.

Simcoe was an ardent Tory and royalist intent on ensuring that republican ideas expressed in the American Revolution not be established in the colony. He believed in a type of aristocratic society dominated by leading families. In time, this led to an oligarchic type of government in which power rested with the Family Compact who controlled the Legislative Council, but in Simcoe's own day the system worked reasonably well.

When John Graves Simcoe came to Upper Canada, he arrived with his wife, Elizabeth, and some of his young children. Elizabeth Simcoe was an artist and diarist who has left us with vivid descriptions of Upper Canada in her time. In 1796, she recorded her impressions of a trip she made with the governor and others along the Niagara Peninsula to the Head of the Lake. The party travelled on horseback to the King's Head Inn, located just south of the Beach Strip, where they met a number of Native people who had assembled to meet the governor.

[They] fired muskets in our horses' faces, their usual mark of respect, which frightened me and my horse very much; he started and I shrieked, but the sound was lost in the whoops of the Indians. They gave us the largest land tortoise I ever saw....

The river and bay were full of canoes; the Indians were fishing; we bought some fine salmon off them. When we had near crossed the bay, [Richard] Beasley's house became a very pretty object. We landed at it and walked up the hill from whence is a beautiful view of the lake, with wooded points breaking the line of shore and Flamborough in the background. The hill is quite like a park with large oak trees dispersed but no underwood.... Further west of this terrace we saw Coote's Paradise, so called from a Captain Coote, who spent a great deal of time in shooting ducks in this marshy tract.... It abounds with wild fowl and tortoises....

I was so pleased with this place that the Governor stayed and dined at Beasley's.... We arrived late and found a salmon and tortoise ready dressed for our dinner.

—Elizabeth Simcoe[7]

Imposing Order onto the Wilderness

Governor Simcoe engaged Augustus Jones, the brother of Mary Gage, to survey the roads of Barton and Saltfleet Townships. This survey, carried out in 1791, imposed a set of roads that continue to shape the landscape of Hamilton and the surrounding area.

Jones began the east–west survey with a baseline along the bay. We now call that baseline Burlington Street. He then laid down the concession roads to the south at 5/8 of a mile intervals. Concession 1 we call Barton Street; 2 is Main Street; concession 3 we still call Concession Street; running along the brow of the mountain, today's Fennell Avenue is concession 4; Mohawk is 5; Limeridge is 6; Stone Church Road is 7; and finally, Highway 53 is concession road 8.

Once Jones had the concession roads surveyed, he surveyed the side roads. They are a half-mile apart and are named Stratherne, Kenilworth, Ottawa, Gage, Sherman, Wentworth,

Wellington, James, Queen, Dundurn, and Longwood. For many years, these roads remained no more than imaginary lines through the bush, but for the British this grid symbolized the imposition of order onto the wilderness, an order that remains today.

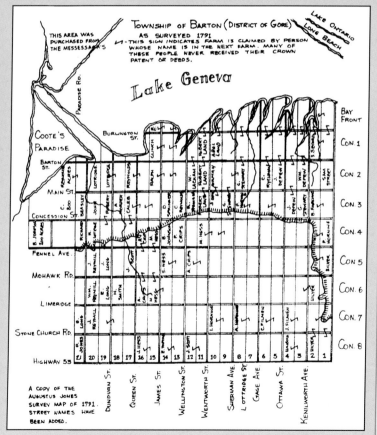

Many water powered mills, for grinding grain or cutting lumber, were built in Upper Canada. The Hamilton area was a particularly good location because of the many streams coming off the Niagara Escarpment.

The ruins of a mill near Greensville.

War on the Niagara Frontier

In the two decades after the arrival of Governor Simcoe the colony of Upper Canada grew and prospered. By 1812, Upper Canada had a population of 77,000. Only 20,000 were Loyalists. The rest were American settlers of questionable loyalty who had crossed the border seeking cheap land.

The days of bare subsistence were over by 1800. The fur trade had retreated to the north and far west, and the major marketable commodity of the area was grain. It was difficult to transport to market and the price was low, but grain was one crop that a farmer could grow to realize some cash. All over the Niagara area, mills driven by waterpower sprang up to grind the grain into flour.

At this time, Ancaster was the largest village at the Head of the Lake. Its location on the brow of the escarpment provided streams that could be harnessed to produce power. By 1795, St. Jean Rousseau, a French Canadian who had been a fur trader at the mouth of the Humber River, owned and operated a saw and grist mill in Ancaster. Taverns and churches were established, and the first school at the Head of the Lake was opened in the village in 1796.

Dundas was originally called King's Landing Place. The town was founded in 1793 when Simcoe ordered that a 60-acre plot be set aside for a town site. It was then called Coote's Paradise and only in 1801 took on the name Dundas Mills. The town was at the junction of a number of important roads and grew as a trading and transportation centre. The Governor's Road went west to London and Windsor. Dundas Street ran east to the capital at York (Toronto), and then continued further east along the lake to Kingston. There were other roads to Waterloo and Guelph. Dundas was the location of the first post office at the Head of the Lake, built in 1814.

Saltfleet Township had already become an important agricultural area. A grist mill at Albion Falls was owned and operated by the Davis family and a flour mill at Stoney Creek was operated by Adam Green, a New Jersey loyalist.

Hamilton was no more than a crossroads at this time. King Street went from Newark in the east to Ancaster in the west, York Street crossed Burlington Heights, and the Beach Road ran from across the Beach Strip to points north and east. In 1795, Smith's Tavern was opened in a log structure at the northwest corner of what was to become King and Wellington

An old postcard showing the mill at Mt. Albion Falls.

Streets. A great deal of heavy drinking took place in that frontier society, but taverns were also one of the few places were people could meet and discuss the business of the day. Smith's Tavern became the meeting place of the Barton Lodge of the Freemasons, an organization in which virtually all of the prominent families participated.

The important issues then, as today, were political. The Loyalists were refugees and they shared vivid memories of being driven out of their homes. They knew that the Americans hated and feared the British and looked towards Canada as both a threat and an opportunity for expansion. The Loyalists recognized they had to be prepared to defend their colony or run the risk of losing their homes yet again.

The British garrisoned a small number of regular troops in Upper Canada, but this force would not be enough to defend the colony in the face of a full scale invasion. The legislature passed the Militia Act in 1793, requiring military service of all males between the ages of 16 and 50. Later, the requirement was expanded to include those up to 60 years of age. All males of military age were required to meet for parade twice a year and they had to bring their own firearms.

When war with the Americans finally came in 1812, the people of the Niagara Peninsula rallied to save their new country. It was a desperate struggle that was almost lost in more than a score of battles. The members of the Loyalist militia made the difference between defeat and victory.

A reenactment of the Battle of Stoney Creek.

The Battle of Stoney Creek

The primary concern of General Isaac Brock, the commanding officer of the British forces in Upper Canada in the first year of the war, was the loyalty of the American settlers. If they were to take up arms and join the Americans forces, their overwhelming numbers would soon swamp the British Army and the Canadian militia. In that first year of the war, Brock launched a brilliant campaign, with his small forces, in Detroit and along the Niagara Frontier — a campaign that defeated the Americans at every turn. The costs were high. Brock lost his life at the Battle of Queenston Heights, but the victories compelled the American settlers to take a wait-and-see attitude toward the war.

The summer campaign of 1813 had a different outcome. The Americans took the capital of York, they dominated the naval campaign on Lake Ontario, and their army crossed the Niagara River and took Fort George at Newark. The British forces abandoned the Niagara Frontier and made an orderly retreat back to the Head of the Lake, where they fortified their headquarters at Burlington Heights.

The British held a strong position. The heights are 250 feet above the lake and surrounded by water on three sides. The soldiers built a defensive wall on the south, but General Vincent, the British Chief of Staff, doubted that they could hold the Heights for long. If they were forced to abandon Burlington Heights, then all of Upper Canada west of Kingston would be lost to the enemy.

The American Army that pursued Vincent and the British numbered 3,000. The British forces at Burlington Heights were only 1,300. Most of them were hardened British regular troops, but there were about 130 Canadian militiamen drawn from Loyalist families in the Niagara Peninsula. The Americans advanced cautiously, and in the late afternoon of June 5 they camped in Stoney Creek on the Gage family farm. The American officers took over the Gage farm house for their headquarters and locked Mary Gage and her family in the basement.

All through that day, the progress of the American Army had been watched by a 19-year-old by the name of Billy Green, whose family owned the mill in Stoney Creek. He heard that a neighbour, Isaac Corman, had been captured and set out to find him. Billy signalled with bird calls, and soon heard Isaac replying with an owl hoot. When they met, Corman told Billy that he had been released because he was a relative of one of the American Generals, but more importantly he had learned the American password. Billy volunteered to take the password to the British at Burlington Heights.

Billy rode on horseback along the mountain and then down the trail to Burlington Heights. When he met the British guards, he demanded to speak to the general. At first, the British soldiers thought he was a spy, but he finally convinced them. Colonel Harvey, the second in command, had already come to the conclusion that to save the situation the British would have to make a surprise attack on the Americans. With Billy's information about the location of the American troops, and the password, Colonel Harvey was convinced that they now had an advantage. General Vincent quickly agreed to the attack.

At 11:30 at night, 704 men set out with Colonel Harvey in command and Billy Green out in front as guide. Silently, they marched down King Street in the dead of night. This is how one of the soldiers remembered it:

I shall never forget the agony caused to the senses by the stealthiness with which we proceeded to the midnight slaughter … not a whisper was permitted; even our footsteps were not allowed to be heard.

—E.B. Biggar

The British on the march at a reenactment of the Battle of Stoney Creek.

American soldiers fire a volley.

artillery; and again the trees, the tents, and everything about lives as in momentary day; and again the whizzing bullets are followed by moans and dying words. But now the flashes come from the flats also, and from simultaneous volleys the firing runs into an incessant roar, the hill and valley are continuous sheets of living flame and the sky is bright with glare.

—E.B. Biggar[8]

It was a fierce but short battle. The Americans became confused, some shot at their own troops, others blundered into the British and were captured. The Gage family, who were huddled in the basement of their house, listened in terror as the battle raged about them. By daybreak it was over. Some 55 Americans were dead or wounded, and 125 officers and men were taken prisoner, including two generals. The British had lost 23 men and 136 had been wounded. By noon, the Americans ordered a withdrawal, abandoning their dead to the British. As they retreated, settlers hidden in the woods gave Indian war whoops, which hastened the Americans along their way.

The Battle of Stoney Creek marked a turning point in the war.

One by one the sentries were removed, and still the American camp was not roused. Then the sudden surprise attack was unleashed.

Following the dreadful flash and crash came a silence yet more impressive, broken by the clinking of ramrods. Now an ominous "click! click! click!" rattles along the gloomy hill, succeeded by another echoing roar of musketry and sock of

This was the furthest incursion of the Americans on the Niagara Peninsula. By the next year, they were pushed back all along the frontier and gradually driven out of Canada altogether. A stalemate emerged that lasted until a peace treaty was signed.

But after the war, one further incident occurred at the Head of the Lake, which indicates the bitterness of the conflict. In a tavern in the town of Ancaster, eight men were convicted of treason for giving information and provisions to the enemy. They were sentenced to be hung, drawn, and quartered. The hanging was carried out just outside the fortifications of Burlington Heights, about where York and Dundurn Streets meet today. John Ryckman was there.

British fortifications built during the War of 1812 can still be seen in the cemetery on Burlington Heights. Tombs of prominent Hamiltonians have been built into the battlements.

Monument commemorating the Battle of Stoney Creek.

There was a rude gallows with eight nooses. Four victims stood in each of two wagons, which had been drawn under the gallows. They stood on boards laid across the wagons while the hangman adjusted the nooses, then the wagons were driven off. As they strangled their contortions loosened the gallows and a heavy brace which came loose, fell and struck one of the victims on the head, killing him instantly. When the others had ceased to struggle their heads were chopped off and exhibited as traitors.

Seven of them had been willing to die but the eighth pleaded for life, saying that he had done it from the feeling of hospitality and had not known whom he was entertaining, but it helped him not at all.[9]

The war had been a desperate struggle for the survival of Upper Canada. When peace came in 1814, the settlers of the colony felt a surge of optimism. They would have to face new challenges and a different form of conflict, but they had withstood the attacks of a much larger and more powerful enemy. In the process, they had built confidence in themselves and in their ability to create a prosperous country.

Chapter Two

A TOWN CALLED HAMILTON
(1814 – 1840)

Once the hostilities were over, the tempo of the young province of Upper Canada increased significantly. The government built roads and canals. Immigration from the British Isles brought new people to settle the rich agricultural lands in the southwest and provided skilled and semi-skilled workers to labour in the growing towns and villages of the colony. But soon a fundamental conflict emerged that pitted an elite, gathered around a few powerful men, called the Family Compact, against a group of farmers and members of the growing middle class who called themselves Reformers.

George Hamilton Comes to the Head of the Lake

George Hamilton was a man who came from the small group of families that Simcoe felt were the natural rulers of this British colony. His father was a merchant and was involved in business dealings with Richard Beasley and others. George had married Maria Jarvis, the daughter of the provincial secretary. During the war, he had distinguished himself in a number of engagements, including the Battle of Queenston Heights and Lundy's Lane.

Hamilton's house in Queenston had been damaged during the

George Hamilton's house, Bellevue, was built prior to the War of 1812 by James Durand.

war, and his family was left homeless. He had served with Captain James Durand, who owned a house and property at the Head of the Lake. Durand decided to pursue business interests in Belleville, and on January 25, 1815, Hamilton bought the Durand house and 257 acres of land for 1,750 pounds. Today, this land is in the heart of the City of Hamilton.

The land was in two parcels. One parcel extended from what is today James Street, east to Mary, and from Main to the mountain. The second took in the block from Main to King Streets, and from James to Mary. The house that Hamilton purchased was a handsome stone structure called Bellevue, with a widow's walk, French doors, and full-length windows. It was located a little east of John Street just under the mountain. Soon after the purchase was completed, Hamilton moved his wife and infant son from York, where they had taken refuge during the war, into their new home.

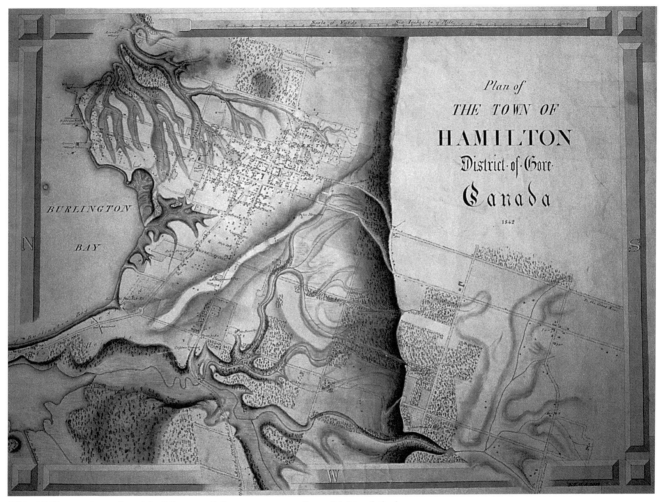

This 1842 map shows the original features of the escarpment, creeks, and inlets of the bay.

Hamilton was a type of real estate developer and shortly after he acquired the land, he surveyed streets, subdivided the land into lots, and put them up for sale. A number of streets were named after members of his family: James, John, and Hunter, after his brothers, and Catherine after his mother. But little happened. Then a political plum dropped into his lap, which, no doubt, was arranged by his friends in government.

The District of Gore and Its Courthouse

Prior to the war, settlers in the area had appealed to the legislature to form a new judicial district so that people would not have to travel long distances when they had to appear in court. James Durand had applied to have his property selected as the centre of the district, and the Town of Dundas had done the same. The legislature was about to make a decision on this issue when the war came along and the proposal was shelved. After the war, it came forward again.

On March 22, 1816, legislation was passed naming the small community, then no more than a handful of people, the judicial centre of the District of Gore, which was made up of the Counties of Wentworth, Halton, Brant, Haldimand, and the Township of Puslinch in the County of Wellington. The people of Dundas were outraged, but there was nothing they could do about it. The legislation went on to state that a courthouse and jail were to be built, and named the community "Hamilton" after its leading citizen. This is how Hamilton got its name.[1]

As part of the arrangements for receiving this political plum, George Hamilton donated two acres of land for the courthouse and jail on Main Street, from Hughson to Catherine. The county courthouse remains in that location to this day. The original jail was built out of hewn logs to the height of 10 feet. It had four rooms: two for prisoners, one for debtors, and the other for the jailor and his family. This is a description of the jail by F.W. Fearman, who grew up in Hamilton in this period:

The jail was extremely strong, so far as the outer walls were concerned but the designer seemed to have entirely overlooked the floors and foundation so it was found necessary to provide the two criminal cells with substantial chains, which

Items in the Hamilton Board of Police Minute Book

1833: By-law No. Three: "Every person convicted of having willfully or negligently suffered his or her hogs, pig or pigs to run at large in the Town of Hamilton, shall be liable to a penalty of five shilling for every such hog so suffered to run at large."

1833: Every dwelling house was required to have a ladder and a "leathern bucket holding not less than three gallons," for fighting fires.

1836: Mr. Oliver, prize boxer, fined 15 shillings on April 24, 1838 (for) holding a gymnastic display in the town.

1836: Mr. Hyatt, brought up for using profane and blasphemous language. Discharged on promising to leave the town.

were securely riveted around the legs of the worst class of prisoners. The others took their departure at such times as seemed to them best by raising a plank of the floor and digging out under the foundation. Numerous escapes were made in this manner.

There was also a pillory and whipping post. Two hours in the pillory or 39 lashes with the cat-of-nine-tails, being the common sentence for rogues who committed small sentences. More serious criminals were banished to the United States.

—F.W. Fearman[2]

A man by the name of Joseph Cole had the distinction of receiving the first sentence. The court records state that he was

Sentenced to be kept in jail till the first day of the next quarter sessions [three months] when, at mid-day, in the town of Hamilton, to be publicly whipped with forty lashes … on the bare back and then discharged.[3]

Four courthouses have stood on the land donated by George Hamilton. The first was a log structure (Below). In 1827, the second (Opposite) was built and on August 17, 1877, the cornerstone for the third was laid (Right). It was demolished in 1956 to make room for the present structure.

As well as donating land for the courthouse, Hamilton donated a triangular piece of property to the community for Gore Park. Nathaniel Hughson, who owned the property to the north of King Street, was to donate a piece of property of equal size and shape to make up an imposing town square, but Hughson later declined this agreement and Gore Park has remained a triangle ever since.

Once the courthouse and jail were functioning, people from across the Gore District who needed to register property and those involved with civil disputes or criminal charges came to Hamilton to have the matters dealt with. Many travelled long distances. Booths were set up on the John Street end of Gore Park dispensing spruce beer, ginger cakes, and apple pies. A haymarket south of the courthouse was established so that travellers would have fodder for their horses. Business developed and the village, focused between King Street in the north and the mountain to the south, James Street in the west and Wellington Street in the east, began to grow.

Soon, other facilities began to develop. Education for children was of utmost importance to the early settlers, and they struggled to provide schools in the area. In 1817, a survey found that five schools were operating in Barton Township, with an estimated enrollment of 800 students. These were semi-private schools of poor quality, but they played an important role in educating this rural population. In 1821, a school opened on the corner of Hughson and Jackson Streets with John Law as headmaster. It was said that Law was "thorough in his teaching, strict in discipline and had an abiding faith in the virtue of the rod."

According to Fearman, children in those days had a wonderful time exploring and playing in a country that had been a wilderness just a short time previously.

Thousands of passenger pigeons would pass overhead, and they could be knocked down by sticks in the hundreds. Splendid duck shooting was to be had on the heights: black duck, mallard, teal, and now and then canvasbacks. Close to the wood market boys had a grand time gathering hickory nuts....

I have seen the Gore filled with long, white-covered emigrant wagons on their way from the eastern states to the far west of Illinois, Western Ohio and Indiana. They would park there for the night with their cattle and horses and sleep in the wagons or prairie schooners as we used to call them, and at the break of day they would be gone. The next evening another group would be resting there.[4]

The Harbour

The courts provided the initial development for the village, but an even greater economic impetus came with the development of the harbour. Originally, the outlet of the bay was a small stream that was so shallow that only canoes or shallow draft boats could pass. The government was keen to improve navigation, and on March 19, 1823, an act was passed in the legislature providing for the construction of a navigable channel to be cut through the Beach Strip to connect the bay with Lake Ontario. It was to be a channel 12 feet in depth, deep enough for the largest of the lake boats.

Etching of the Hamilton wharves and grain elevator.

In 1823, work was begun on the canal. It was completed in 1826, but from the moment it was opened it was deemed inadequate. In 1827, a new survey was made and work was begun to deepen and widen the canal. It was finally completed in 1832, at the cost of $94,000. A seventy-foot swing bridge was built across the canal, but it was soon destroyed by a schooner and for many years a scow ferry took people across the channel.

The canal was a big project for the day, and much of the labour was done by pick and shovel. Workmen flocked to the area. Many set up ramshackle houses along the bay front in what we now call the North End. Soon there were storehouses, barns for horses, and boathouses. Once the canal opened a large wharf for steamboats was built at the foot of James Street and smaller wharves were built along the shoreline.

Hamilton now had one community that stretched south of King to the mountain and a second along the waterfront. The two communities were separated by a marsh, with James Street North, a corduroy road, connecting them. But more than geography separated the two communities. By the early nineteenth century, the North End was already inhabited by people distinctly different from their more staid neighbours who lived closer to the mountain. This is how a North Ender described the characters of his community in that day:

A rough tough reckless lot, hard working, hard playing, hard living, hard swearing, hard drinking ... the liveliest, loveliest part of Hamilton, set apart by the neighbourliness and fierce pride of its people, home of cockfights, good times and a legion of the city's most colourful characters.

—David M. Nelligan[5]

A building originally used for cockfighting on the Dundurn Castle grounds.

When the improved canal was opened, steam ships began to make regular stops at Hamilton, and several schooners that hauled cargo to different ports around Lake Ontario operated out of the bay. The traffic in the harbour grew rapidly, and the export of grain from the developing agricultural lands to the west began.

Allan Napier MacNab

During this early period, no one was as closely identified with Hamilton and its development as Allan Napier MacNab. MacNab's father was a military man who came to Canada as one of Lieutenant-Governor Simcoe's aides. Although his father had little money during his life, and may in fact have been in debtor's prison when Allan

Napier was born, he boasted that he was a direct descendent of the Laird of MacNab. When the War of 1812 broke out, Allan was only 14 years old. He joined the navy and distinguished himself to the extent that he earned the reputation as "boy hero."

After the war, Allan MacNab worked at various jobs around the capital of York and undertook legal training, but his fortunes rose and fell. By 1821, he was well off enough to be married, but by 1824 he was bankrupt. In 1826, he moved to Hamilton, a town that only had 200 inhabitants, and was called to the bar that year, enabling him to practise law. Soon his fortunes took a turn for the better. By the early 1830s, MacNab had become the most important businessman in the district. His law practice thrived, he owned several properties in the town and around the province, and he was the president or director of all of the important companies in Hamilton. This is how one of his friends described him:

Above the middle size, well proportioned, sparkling eyes with a handsome and intelligent countenance and brisk air … a lively wit, a considerable share of good humour and a devil may care manner … excessively fond of perpetuating practical jokes.

—Edward Ermatinger[6]

But not everyone agreed with this sunny assessment. MacNab was a political figure, and in that day of fiercely partisan politics the judgment of a man depended on his politics. MacNab's enemies described him as a "bully boy," or the "Bully of York Tories," a "super loyalist," or "a political meddler and upstart."

By the late 1820s, politics had become fiercely partisan in Upper Canada. An intense competition had developed between the Tories, who supported the oligarchic Family Compact, and the Reformers, who advocated responsible government and control by the people through an elected parliament. MacNab had come from

Sir Allan MacNab

a Tory family and he remained a Tory by both tradition and political instinct all of his life.

Shortly after he arrived in Hamilton, MacNab was named as one of the people involved in the tar and feathering of the lawyer George Rolph of Dundas. Rolph and his brother, Dr. John Rolph, were leading Reformers in the area, and Dundas was known as a Reform town. Allegations were made that Rolph was tar and feathered because he had an affair with his housekeeper, but most believed that this was a Tory attempt to intimidate a member of the opposition.[7]

In 1829, an even more notorious political event created uproar in the colony. The Reformers held the majority in the Legislature, and a Hamilton group of Tories hung the Lieutenant-Governor, Sir John Colbourn, in effigy in an attempt to embarrass them. The Reformers wanted to ensure that they were not blamed for this outrage and called Allan MacNab to the bar of the legislature, demanding that he reveal the names of those involved. MacNab refused and was imprisoned for 10 days for his silence. When he emerged from jail, he was proclaimed a hero. MacNab had become the leader of the Tories in the Hamilton area. He stood for election as the member for Wentworth in 1830 and was easily elected. He retained his seat for 30 years.

Dundurn Castle

For a man such as MacNab, with ambitions to establish a noble family lineage in the new world, it was very important to have a house worthy of his prestige as a gentleman and leader of the North American branch of the Clan MacNab. By the 1830s, Richard Beasley, who had long resided at his stone home on Burlington Heights, was in deep financial trouble. He lost the house, and the 500 acres that went with it, to the person who held the mortgage, and in 1832 Allan MacNab bought this property for 2,500 pounds.

Over the next two years MacNab, along with the young architect Robert Charles Wetherall, built Dundurn. It remains one of the finest buildings of its era in North America. We call Dundurn a castle because of its impressive size, but in fact it is a regency villa, built in the style of early nineteenth-century British manor houses. Every opportunity was used to impress.

Beasley had chosen the best location for his house. The British Army had commandeered the house in the War of 1812, and it is believed they built an underground cellar or vault in the basement to store their armaments. Wetherall decided to incorporate the Beasley stone cottage into Dundurn to take advantage of the location. Remains of the cottage are in the centre block of Dundurn, and the armament warehouse is still preserved beneath it.

Dundurn Castle was built by Sir Allan MacNab, who came to Hamilton to practise law in 1826.

Postcard of Dundurn Castle in 1890s, shortly after the area became a park.

The wings of Beasley's house were demolished, and much larger wings were built. Long French windows were placed so that the garden could be seen from inside the house.

During this period, MacNab's family was expanding. His first wife had died, and he remarried and had three young children by his second wife. Two of his sisters were also part of the household. Dundurn was designed so that the family could grow up in comfortable surroundings while he continued operating his business and political affairs out of the residence. The wings held self-contained suites of apartments for the family.

Left: *The original kitchen of Dundurn Castle.*
Right Inset: *Dundurn Castle.*

The house could also accommodate formal ceremonial occasions with ease and grace, as was expected from a man of MacNab's social standing. The large drawing room and library could be isolated from the rest of the house, and the formal dining room provided a lavish setting for entertaining. The grounds of the estate, which today make up Dundurn Park, remain one of the best features of the whole complex. A number of outbuildings also remain on the property. The Battery Lodge, which was recently moved to widen York Street, is thought to have been used as a gun emplacement during the War of 1812. The "Poultry House" was used for cock fighting, a popular activity of the day.

Dundurn remains an impressive building, but to the people of MacNab's day it must have appeared to be from a world beyond their imaginations. Poverty was widespread among the population. The possibility of economic disaster was imminent for farmers and townspeople alike. But what was feared most of all were those disasters and epidemics over which people had no control.

Epidemics and Fires

In the summer of 1832, the same year that MacNab bought the property at Burlington Heights, tragedy struck the city. Cholera: The very word struck fear into the people of Upper Canada. The town rushed to clean up its garbage and disinfect its outhouses, but it did little good. Hamilton was a port, and immigrants who had been trapped in the holds of ships for weeks arrived carrying the deadly disease. The following resolution was passed on June 23, 1832.

The Lieutenant Governor requests that you will take immediate measures for causing all vessels bound for the port of Burlington Bay or Hamilton to be visited by a person authorized by the Board of Health in order that the infected person on board may be disposed of as the Board may think fit.

But these measures did little to placate the panic that spread through the population. Schooners pulling into the wharfs in the North End with immigrants aboard were met by citizens armed with pitchforks.

Still, the authorities did what they could to try to help those infected by the disease. George Hamilton, the town's founder, persuaded his fellow citizens to build shelters on the shore of the bay for the immigrants. An old stone barracks at Burlington Heights, dating from the War of 1812, became a hospital, and wagonloads of dead and nearly dead people were transported there. Those that died were covered in quicklime and quickly buried in the growing cemetery on Burlington Heights. Even the prisoners in the jail were released, to give them a chance to escape the cholera epidemic, when George Hamilton, Allan MacNab, and others stood surety for them. But the number of dead mounted.

Cholera struck many immigrants brought to Canada in the holds of ships.

This is an account of a recently arrived immigrant who experienced those difficult days:

On enquiry it was found impossible to procure a dwelling house on account of our having passed through the cholera district. The immigrant shed in the northeastern part of the town seemed too filthy to enter. By the time that we reached the wharf on our return, Bella Little had been seized by the cholera and died. The solemn but small funeral procession left the wharf about four o'clock in the afternoon and the corpse was laid in mother earth at the Methodist church on the corner of King and Wellington Streets, the only public burying ground in the town at the time. On our return to our headquarters at the wharf Mr. Gunn and his clerk, Mr. Vallance, took pity on us and kindly had us placed in the storehouse under cover. Mr. George Little, who had just married his young wife before leaving Scotland and who seemed to be in perfect health when he returned from the mournful rite performed to the remains of his deceased sister, was taken sick at ten o'clock that night and died at two o'clock next morning.

—John Glasgow[8]

Another story of a Hamilton family relates how a seven year old girl, "recently arrived by ship in this foreign land, lay wide-eyed in the night listening to the ominous chant of the town crier: 'Bring out your dead! Bring out your dead!'"[9]

Thankfully, as the cold weather set in the epidemic began to wane, but in November of that year fire stuck in a new tavern owned by Allan MacNab in the center of town. By the time it was put out,

Firemen showing off their mid-19th century equipment.

six buildings had been destroyed before the citizen bucket brigade brought it under control.

Hamilton had no organized fire department, but every stalwart citizen was supposed to have a bucket hanging convenient to his home and when the cry of fire was heard in the streets, say about midnight, when the thermometer was trying to turn itself upside down, and dropping to thirty or forty degrees below zero, half dressed men by the score could be seen running from every direction, bucket in hand, towards where the sky was lurid and the flames lapping up the home of some unfortunate. Those were the days when excited men, anxious to be of some use to their unfortunate neighbours, would throw furniture and looking glasses out of upper windows of the burning houses and carry out some trifling article of no intrinsic value.[10]

But not everything resulted in disaster in the early 1830s. Immigration from Britain swelled the population of Upper Canada. In 1826, the population of Barton Township was 1,195. By 1835, the Town of Hamilton alone was more than 2,600. On January 8, 1833, an act was passed in the legislature to create the Police Village of Hamilton. The boundaries were Wellington Street in the east, Queen in the west, the bay in the north, and Concession Street in the south. Four wards were created, with King Street and John Street as the dividing lines. The first election was a relatively modest affair. Only 46 people voted. Not surprisingly, the first order of business of the newly formed town was fire protection.

The Desjardins Canal

The first half of the nineteenth century was the era of canal building in Canada. Visionaries of the day saw the St. Lawrence and Great Lakes as a natural system of transportation, and canals were built to overcome the obstacles. The canal through the Beach Strip, which separated the bay from Lake Ontario, was part of that vision, and a French immigrant who had settled in Dundas by the name of Pierre Desjardins had an even bigger dream that would favour his adopted town.

As early as 1820, Desjardins petitioned the government to grant him land so that he could dig a canal from the bay, through Coote's Paradise, to the town of Dundas. His petition was granted and a joint stock company was established and authorized to raise money by the selling of shares; this was one of the first public companies in Upper Canada. Once he had the land, Desjardins entered into a contract with a Mr. Whyte to dig a canal seven feet wide and four feet deep. "The cost of digging was set at $1.00 per rod, and Desjardins bound

Colourized postcard of the turning basin in Dundas, at the head of the Desjardins Canal. In the 1840s, the basin was lined with warehouses.

After the Desjardins Canal was opened, Dundas became the busiest port on Lake Ontario for a period.

It was in those days that the sight of from 12 to 15 large masted boats — grain, lumber and general carriers from seaport places on the St. Lawrence River — gathered in the canal basin was no uncommon thing. In those days the shores of the basin were lined with great warehouses where grain and other products were stored for shipment. From Galt, Guelph, Preston and all the other inland centers in Dundas direction the farmers brought their stuff to the canal for shipment, and it was not uncommon sight in the busy season to see as many as a hundred teams toiling down King Street through the town to the warehouses at the canal. It was also to be the headquarters for importation by water and many a load of emigrants first set foot on Canadian soil from the basin wharves. Many of the poor wretches too died about there and their bones to the number of several hundred bodies mingle with the dust of cholera victims.[13]

the bargain by delivering to Mr. Whyte 1 case of goods and 1 barrel of whiskey, whiskey being a shilling a gallon in those days."[11]

Desjardins died in 1827 and never saw his canal completed, but others carried on the work. Allan MacNab became involved and used his political influence to obtain loans from the government. George Hamilton and a number of others became investors. The work went slowly, but the Desjardins Canal Company was set up, considerable sums of money were raised, the work progressed, and then …

Finally on the 16th of August 1837 the Desjardins Canal opened. Banners were flying from the steamer Argylle *as she sailed down the canal from Dundas … into the bay and back … aboard her … all the while a brass band played lively military music. That evening there was a dinner held in Bamberger's Dundas … in celebration of the opening, and following the dinner there was an official Desjardins Canal Ball.[12]*

A mill on Spencer Creek in Dundas.

Dundas grew to be a prosperous milling town with grist and saw mills, a distillery, tannery, woolen mill, newspaper, and iron foundry. Admittedly, there were problems. The main streets of town were lined with saloons and hotels well-frequented by patrons. One traveller claimed that, while the trip from Hamilton to Galt took four days, two of those days were needed to get through Dundas. But in that day of heavy drinking of hard liquor, the town was little different than others on the frontier.

Rebellion

Through the 1830s, political conflict kept Upper Canada

Riley House was a hotel and stagecoach post in Dundas. Even after the coming of the railways, stagecoaches remained an important mode of travel.

oratorical flair. Mackenzie had a broad following across Upper Canada, particularly in rural areas.

MacNab was elected to the legislature in 1830, and soon proved to be an able parliamentarian. Seated across from him was Mackenzie, a spellbinding speaker but known to be wild and unpredictable. "Once the two met as politicians they became bitter antagonists. They shared a certain largeness of spirit and a pronounced tendency to personalize political issues. Beyond that they were opposites in almost every way."[14]

It was MacNab who led the attack against Mackenzie in the legislature

in turmoil and the people of this area were in the thick of it. Dundas and Hamilton were of about equal size at the time. Dundas was a Reform town, led by the Rolph brothers, and Hamilton supported the Family Compact, which was led by Allan MacNab, the arch Tory.

For a number of years, the conflict was focused on the legislature of Upper Canada. The Tories supported the ruling oligarchy that controlled the Executive Council, while members of what were called the Reform Group were the opposition. The most outspoken and radical of that group was William Lyon Mackenzie, who had lived in Dundas when he first came to Canada between 1820 and 1822. Mackenzie was the publisher and editor of a newspaper called the *Colonial Advocate*. He was a Scot with a quick temper and brilliant

in the early 1830s by demanding his expulsion. Three times he won a vote and the firebrand was expelled, but each time he ran for re-election in the riding of York and won a majority again. In August 1835, just as the MacNabs were moving into their new home of Dundurn Castle, the contest took on an even more bitter tone. Mackenzie accused Allan MacNab in the legislature of owing money to the Gore Bank while being a director of the company. MacNab was furious; he proclaimed his innocence and denounced his accusers, but this did not stop Mackenzie. Rumours circulated that Reformers were going to burn down MacNab's new mansion.

The political temper of the time was exacerbated by an economic downturn.

In '34 and '36 business was bad, no money, prices were low. All trade and no truck; no cash for anything. The shopkeepers used to print their own shinplasters and each ran a bank of his own until the government put a stop to it. Wages were very low. A labouring men got 50 cents to 75 cents a day or less and mechanics not much more, paid in truck. Prices were low … General discontent prevailed.

—F.W. Fearman [15]

The new Lieutenant-Governor, Sir Francis Bond Head, intervened on the side of the Tories in the 1836 election, and the Tories won a majority in the legislature. Many of the more moderate Reform voices withdrew temporarily from the political fray, but not Mackenzie. Using his new paper, *The Constitution*, he constantly attacked the government and Bond Head. Meetings of Reform groups all across the southwest of the colony denounced the government. The province was in an uproar. Finally, on December 4, 1837, a group of rebels gathered at Montgomery's Tavern on Yonge Street, north of Toronto and prepared to march on the capital to oust the government.

On hearing this, MacNab sprang into action. He mounted his favourite horse, Sam Patch, gathered 60 Hamilton men who supported the government — the "Men of Gore," they came to be called — commandeered the steamship *Traveler*, and headed for the battlefront. Once the men arrived in the capital, a meeting at the Town Hall declared MacNab the saviour of the city. Bond Head wanted to appoint him the Commander-in-Chief of the government forces, but deferred to Colonel James FitzGibbon. Placing the Men of Gore in the vanguard of the little army, they marched up Yonge Street, and after a few shots the rebels scattered. Later, MacNab rode at the head of the main column as they approached Montgomery's Tavern, but the leaders of the revolt had already vanished.

The turmoil was to go on for months. Mackenzie escaped on horseback, heading west. There was a reward of 1,000 pounds on his head, and troops searched for the fiery rebel, but no one betrayed him. Travelling at night and in disguise, Mackenzie went through Dundas, where Reformer friends helped him. On the mountain, Jacob Rymal, a well-known farmer and later a Member of Parliament gave him a horse and shelter and sent him on his way to the Niagara frontier.

When Allan MacNab got back to Hamilton, rumours were circulating about a rebel force gathering in Brantford. Again, MacNab rallied the Men of Gore and they marched off to do battle, but by the time they got to Brantford the enemy had vanished.

When Mackenzie got across the American border, he established a provisional government on Navy Island, in the middle of the Niagara River. When word of this reached MacNab, he gathered a force together and again marched off into the fray.

When he and his men arrived at the riverbank, they camped out and stared across at Navy Island. Mackenzie and his group were supplied by an American steamer named *Caroline*. On New Year's Eve, a group of Canadians serving under MacNab boarded the *Caroline*, and, after a struggle in which one of the American crew was killed, the vessel was set afire and released into the current.

MacNab was criticized for his role in the burning of the *Caroline* and the Americans protested, but for his efforts in putting down the rebellion he was knighted and received a sword of honour from the legislature. From that time on he was known as Sir Allan Napier MacNab.

William Lyon Mackenzie and his dream of the Republic of Canada had been defeated by his nemesis, the Tory royalist from Hamilton, and yet the struggle for responsible government and a democratic society was not over. The years ahead would open the floodgates to change, and curiously Sir Allan MacNab would become the major agent of change in Hamilton through his promotion of the railway.

William Lyon Mackenzie

Chapter Three

THE RAILROAD TOWN
(1840 – 1865)

I n the year 1836, Dr. Thomas Rolph of Ancaster, a member of the
prominent Rolph family of Reformers, went on a walking tour of
Upper Canada. This is what he wrote about Hamilton:

*There are few places in North America that have increased more rapidly, or
stand in a more beautiful and advantageous situation than the town of
Hamilton. In the summer of 1833, my constant evening's walk was from
McBurley's tavern to the lake shore — distance about one mile. There were
then but two houses between them; now (1836) it is one continued street,
intersected by side streets, branching in both directions.[1]*

The Ambitious Little City

Hamilton was developing at an astounding pace in the 1830s, and
after the depression of the late '30s and early '40s it grew even more
rapidly. By 1840, the town was the largest and most important centre
south and west of Toronto. It was soon calling itself "The Ambitious
Little City."

The most important market for Canadian goods in the early part
of the nineteenth century was Great Britain. A system called the
Corn Laws had grown up, which gave products originating in the

*Great Western Railway engine #51. "N.G." on the front of the engine indicates that
it's narrow gauge.*

Empire a lower rate of tariff as they entered the British market. The
Corn Laws were gradually changed and then abolished altogether in

1846 as Britain adopted a policy of free trade. Canadians were alarmed, predicting economic ruin for the colony, but soon it became apparent that this drop in British trade was more than compensated for by the increase in trade to the United States.

Hamilton was in an excellent position to take advantage of this trade. The first steamboat on Lake Ontario was launched in 1819, and by the 1830s these vessels were making regular stops in the harbour and connecting the town to ports on both the Canadian and the American sides of the lake. The Desjardins Canal to Dundas soon proved to be too narrow and shallow for the larger steamships that were coming to dominate the Lake Ontario trade. The channel through Coote's Paradise also tended to silt up. Hamilton, with its deep harbour and good docking facilities, became the entranceway for goods and people heading further west

These handsome stone townhouses, called Sandyford Place, on the corner of Duke and MacNab Streets, were constructed in the mid 1850s.

Flyer announcing the opening of the Desjardins Canal in 1837.

and it became an important port for the export of agricultural products — particularly wheat — which were being sold to markets to the east.

Hamilton also became linked with other centers by stagecoach lines. In 1835, William Weller established the Telegraph Line of Stage Coaches that ran between Hamilton and Toronto, and in 1842 he renamed it the Royal Mail Stage Coach Line. Four horses pulled each of his stages, and his coaches were painted with the Royal Coat of Arms. Every 15 miles or so the coach would stop at a tavern for refreshments and to change horses. The driver would announce his arrival by blowing on a horn.

Transportation was a key to the development of Hamilton, but enormous problems remained. At this time, southwestern Ontario was

Robert Whale, General View of Hamilton *in 1853. Whale was an outstanding landscape painter who lived in the area.*

The roads were throughout so incredibly bad that no words can give you an idea of them. We often sank in mud holes above the axle; then over trunks of trees laid across swamps, called corduroy roads, where my poor bones dislocated. A wheel here and there or a broken shaft lying by the roadside, told of former wrecks and disasters.... My hands were swelled and blistered by continually grasping with all my strength an iron bar in the front of my vehicle to prevent myself from being flung out.[2]

By the 1840s, Hamilton had developed a number of hotels to serve the needs of travellers, but they were hardly comfortable. A traveller writing under the name of Rubio gave this description in 1842: "Hamilton is a thriving, well situated but drunken town at the head of Lake Ontario.... Everything appeared rough, prosperous, cheap and abundant." In 1844, Robert Godley described the town as "One mass of rubbish and dirt." There, he

the most isolated part of eastern North America. This is a description by a traveller journeying west in 1837:

found an inn and spent the night in a dirty bedroom without any window, where "he managed to sleep pretty well in spite of the fleas."[3]

But despite these problems, the city was beginning to change. Hamilton already had a few industries, though most were small-scale operations run by artisans, but one grew into a large national corporation. Hugh Cossart Baker came to Hamilton in 1843 to work in the Hamilton branch of the Bank of Montreal. He decided that he needed personal insurance and because there was no insurance company in Canada West he travelled all the way to New York City by horseback, stagecoach, and steamboat to meet with a company that might insure him. However, the company turned him down, claiming that because of the climatic hazard of living in Canada and the danger of losing his scalp to "Indians" he was too great a risk. When Baker got back to Hamilton, after his fruitless 1,000-mile trip, he decided to establish his own insurance company. He gathered together prominent Hamilton businessmen and in 1847 a charter was issued to the group for the first insurance company in the province, called the Canada Life Assurance Company. It continues to operate to this day.

Whitehern, an elegant cut-stone mansion on Jackson St., was built in the 1840s. It became the McQuesten family home and is now a museum. It holds many of the original family furnishings and possessions.

A City of Diversity

Up until the early 1840s, Hamilton was almost exclusively a town of Anglo Saxon Protestants. A high percentage of residents were recent British immigrants. Most made an easy transition from the old country to the new because they spoke the same language and shared the same religion and political beliefs. They quickly found jobs and some were accepted into the business elite.

During the Irish famine in the 1840s, many immigrants traveled to Cork to take passage to North America.

had little or no education and few skills. What work the men could get was usually as poorly paid, unskilled labourers, while most of the women became domestic servants. The Irish came to live in the poorest parts of town. Some lived in the North End, close to the docks, but a large number came to live in a neighbourhood called Corktown, an area roughly south of Main Street to Charlton and east of John Street. Young Street was the main road and Catharine Street the

The 1840s marks the beginning of one of the great crises of the nineteenth century: the Irish famine. There had already been considerable migration from Ireland to North America, but when blight hit the potato crop in 1846 poor peasants in the hundreds of thousands fled to North America. Many came by ship up the St. Lawrence canal system and arrived in Hamilton on lake steamers. In 1847, in one week alone 739 immigrants arrived at the docks: most were penniless, many were sick.[4]

By 1846, fully one-third of Hamilton's population was Irish. A large number were young, and unlike the English and Scots, most

Old stone rowhouses in Corktown neighbourhood.

Escaped slaves who came north on the Underground Railway swelled the Black population of Hamilton in the mid-19th century.

A house on Augusta St. in Corktown.

very heart of Corktown.

Hamilton was a reasonably tolerant town for that period, but two incidents suggest that at best there was an uneasy peace between the Irish and the rest of the population. In 1848, the *Spectator* reported that a Corktown man had called out "God bless the Pope." Rocks were thrown, a shot was fired, and a man named Green was hit in the chest.[5] In 1849, during the Orangemen's Parade, 150 men took to the streets, armed with muskets, pistols and swords. The Catholics used pitchforks to defend themselves.[6]

Another group that came to Hamilton during this period comprised African Americans. Slavery had been illegal in Canada since the days of Simcoe, and as early as the 1830s escaped slaves were travelling north to Canada via the Underground Railroad. These people suffered great hardships and dangers and were helped by Whites and Blacks along the way. When they arrived in Canada, it is reported, many fell on their knees and kissed the soil, knowing they had finally reached freedom and safety.

The Black community settled along Concession Street on the mountain and they worked at a variety of jobs throughout the city. By the end of the 1840s, two churches served the community. Although these escaped slaves had gained their freedom in Upper Canada, they found they were still denied the right of public education for their children. In 1843, they sent a petition to the Governor General, asking for permission to send their children to school. Their request was granted, and a law was passed ending this type of discrimination.[7]

Worker's cottage on Caroline St. South, built in the mid-19th century.

Tensions still existed, but the people in Hamilton displayed more tolerance than those in other centres. When the Black Abolitionist Society protested its exclusion from a procession, the organizers of the next festivities placed them not only in the procession but also near its head, before any of the other ethnic societies. Accounts commented that they marched "resplendent in white hats."[8] Every August 1, they celebrated the 1833 anniversary when slavery was formally abolished in the British Empire.

By the 1850s, Hamilton had changed remarkably. The 1851 census found that only 9 per cent of Hamilton's workforce had been born in Canada West. Twenty-nine per cent were from England and Wales, 18 per cent from Scotland, 32 per cent from Ireland, and 8 per cent from the United States. People of all classes lived close together. Some ethnic ghettos developed, like Corktown and the Black community along Concession Street, but they were uncharacteristic. Along the same street could be poor, middle class, and affluent people.

The City of Hamilton

Hamilton grew during the 1840s and 1850s in part because new political arrangements had emerged that went some distance to resolving the discord of the 1830s. After the Rebellion of 1837, the British government sent Lord Durham over to inquire into the causes of the disturbances. His report has come down to us as one of the fundamental documents in the making of the Canadian nation. Durham recommended two major changes: the union of Upper and Lower Canada into one political unit, and responsible government where people, through their elected parliament, would have real control over the government.

Leaders such as Sir Allan MacNab were decidedly unhappy with these proposals. MacNab was a royalist, and conservative to the bone. He felt that any action that reduced the power of the crown and the prerogatives of the legislative council must be opposed on principle, and yet he, and other Conservatives such as John A. Macdonald who arrived on the political scene in this decade, adapted very well to responsible government.

The Reform Group was in power through much of the 1840s, but MacNab retained considerable influence and power. His name is attached to almost every project of substance that was carried out in Hamilton in this decade. He played a key role in representing local interests to the government and using his influence to arrange and fix things in the area. That made him a very valuable person to companies and groups in the community.

In the 1840s, legislation was passed that reorganized local government in Canada West, creating the county system much as it exists today, and on June 9, 1846, Hamilton, a robust, bustling centre

Veterans of the Volunteer Fire Brigade of Hamilton with their 1843 fire "engine."

of 6,832 people, was incorporated into a city. The boundaries were Emerald Street in the east, Paradise Road in the west, Aberdeen in the south and the bay in the north. Five wards were created, and two aldermen were to be elected in each ward. The first mayor was Colin Ferrie, a prosperous local merchant.

The construction of the first city hall had begun in 1836. It was delayed because of the political troubles of 1837, but was completed in 1838. The order of business of the new city council was to deal with things like fire protection, the police, and paving of streets. The first gaslights in the town were turned on in 1851. Health was perhaps the most important issue. The first hospital on Burlington Heights that housed cholera victims had closed. In 1848, for a brief time a

An artist's view of Hamilton in 1854.

Stone rowhouses on James St. South that have been converted into shops.

the city. In the nineteenth century, the poor had to depend on the charity of the rich. The Ladies' Benevolent Society, led by prominent women such as Lydia Jackson, Mary Roach, and Harriet Juson, dispensed bread, coal, and groceries to those who were called the "worthy poor." They cooked soup in a large boiler donated by the industrialist Calvin McQuesten, which provided "the means of nourishing many poor families on a very small outlay." In 1849, a depression year, one in ten Hamilton families received help from the society.[9]

Sports, Culture and Education

As the town grew, more activities became available. Even by the 1840s Hamilton was a sports-crazy town. Not surprisingly, cricket was the most popular sport, since a large part of the population grew up in the British Isles, but people also engaged in a number of other activities. The Young Canadian Baseball Team was organized in Hamilton in 1854, long before many in the United States had ever heard of the sport. Lacrosse was also popular. Sailing and rowing took place on the bay during the summer and, in winter, once the bay was frozen, there was skating, curling, and ice fishing.

temporary hospital was established in a house on Catherine Street and in that year council decided to build a new hospital just below the mountain on Cherry Street (today Ferguson Avenue).

The hospital was also a House of Industry or Poor House, where indigent people with no other support would receive some help from

For the first time, cultural activities came to play an important role. As early as 1837 an amateur band was established. Five years later, the first concert by a professional musician was held. A Segnor Nagel, "the first violinist to the King of Sweden and a pupil of Paganini," gave a concert in the Town Hall. Hamilton had its touring musicians, but by the mid 1850s the city had its own orchestra and chorus. On March 13, 1855, they gave a concert in the Mechanics' Hall on James Street North that was highlighted by Haydn's *Surprise* Symphony.[10] The Hamilton and Gore Mechanics' Institute was established in 1839, with Sir Allan MacNab as the Honourary Patron. The Institute's building on James Street North had a lending library and a 1,000-seat auditorium for public lectures and concerts.

Etching of horse racing on the ice of Hamilton Bay, about 1850.

Another Hamilton institution that was born in the flush of development in the 1840s was the *Spectator*. The city already had three other newspapers, and over the course of Hamilton's history the city has been home to over twenty papers, but the *Spectator* has been the one that has survived and prospered. In 1846, a group of Hamilton business people persuaded Robert Smiley to leave Montreal and come to Hamilton to start the newspaper. Their purpose was to ensure that their Conservative political point of view was heard. With Smiley as the publisher, editor, and principal writer, the newspaper soon became the leading journal of the city. Tragically, he died of tuberculosis in 1855 at the age of 38, but the newspaper carried on under the leadership of his brothers and others.

The rising number of newspapers and books that were circulating reflects the increased literacy and higher levels of education during this time. From the time of the Loyalists, the population of Upper Canada placed a high value on education, but it was difficult in the frontier communities to develop the resources to give good schooling. For most children at this time, the experience of education was a one-room schoolhouse where an overworked teacher taught all subjects to all pupils. Teachers were paid, if at all, out of a share of the district school fund. Not all children attended school, and few would attend much beyond their fourteenth birthday.

Affluent families could afford to send their children to private schools. For example, the Burlington Academy of Hamilton in 1847, located at the corner of Bay and King Streets, had spacious grounds with ornamental shade trees, shrubbery, and flowers. It was described as a "Literary Institution for young ladies with facilities for acquiring an intellectual and moral education." The Academy taught courses in reading, writing, and French, along with painting, embroidery, waxing flowers, etiquette and manners.[11]

In 1847 a proposal came forward to build a

Clock tower of Central Public School, opened in 1853.

A baseball game in 1866.

number of additional one-room schoolhouses, which provoked a debate in the city. At the core of this debate was whether Hamilton schools should adopt the model advocated by the leading Canadian educational reformer of the day, Egerton Ryerson. He believed that schools should have grades in which students would be placed according to their abilities, as well as a standard curriculum and

The Custom House on Stuart Street, near the railway yards and docks, was built in the 1850s. It was recently renovated and now is used as the Ontario Workers' Arts and Heritage Centre.

The Dream of Railways

If there was one single development that converted Hamilton from being a remote city on the edge of the frontier into an important industrial centre, it was the railway. Dreams of railways were at the centre of the nineteenth-century belief in progress. People understood that railways would break the rural isolation, move passengers with unbelievable speed, and bring the produce of the countryside to market and the products of the cities to rural areas. A railway running through a town meant a future of wealth and unbridled growth. Without a railway, it was believed a community faced stagnation and economic decline.

Like others, the people of Hamilton were caught up in this dream. The transportation system of steamships on the Great Lakes and the St. Lawrence was slow and ice bound for five months of the year. The only way to travel into the interior was by wagon and stagecoach over impossible roads. The railway would change all of this, as S. B. Freeman noted in August, 1849:

teachers that could specialize on particular subjects and grades. All these were new ideas that were not readily accepted.

The decision was finally made to adopt these reforms and to build one school for the city rather than a number of one-room schools in different districts. Central Public School was built on Hunter Street West. It opened in May 1853 with 600 students, and was at that time the first graded public school in Canada. It continues to operate to this day.

Every person acquainted with the position of Hamilton must be aware that without this road it would remain an inland town with little commerce and manufactures, but if this railroad were once constructed, Hamilton would be the great mart for the business of the west, as well as for a large portion of the United States.[12]

As early as 1834, Allan MacNab and others tried to raise money for the London and Gore Railway. A charter for the railway was issued by the legislature, but with the onset of the depression and the political troubles it was impossible to secure the financing. By 1845, the group had changed the name to the Great Western Railway, MacNab was made the president, and they proposed to bring the railway from Niagara Falls, through Hamilton, Brantford, London, Chatham, and Windsor.

The line was designed to bring products of the rural areas to

The railway station on Stuart St., in Hamilton's North End. In the early days of railroads, there was always great excitement when the train pulled into town.

Hamilton for shipping through the harbour, but would also connect with other railways east through New York State to New York City and the Eastern Seaboard and west to Detroit, Chicago, and the rapidly developing American Midwest of Ohio, Illinois, and the Mississippi River Valley. The advantage of this route for the Americans was that going through Ontario instead of going south of Lake Erie would cut off 200 kilometres between New York and Chicago. This was a project worthy of dreamers, and Hamilton was at the centre of it all.

Financing the Dream

The problem was not the technology or engineering; it was how to finance this mammoth project. This was where Sir Allan MacNab came in. "Railways are my politics," the old Tory once said, and he meant literally that he intended to use his prestige and political position to get public and government support for his railway projects.

At first, those promoting the railway attempted to raise the money from the public with the sale of shares. The first Hamilton meeting to promote the sale of railroad stock was held in the wood market at Gore Park. An ox was roasted for the occasion, but as Fearman wryly commented, "It was as raw as an east wind." The public offering was equally a failure. A substantial number of people invested in the company, but there was simply not enough money in the country to finance such a huge undertaking.

MacNab then turned to England, a country that at this time was the financial centre of the world. The English, through the London financial markets, were investing in railways on almost every continent. MacNab worked through another Hamilton politician/businessman, Isaac Buchanan, and made connections with a group of capitalists who were willing to invest in the project. MacNab collected a fee of 5,000 pounds for arranging this transaction. When this information later became public, many Hamilton investors felt that this fee was excessive and called for a public inquiry.

Although these private investments in the Great Western were important, the amount of money that was raised was not nearly enough to build the railway. MacNab and others knew that government subsidies were the only answer. The old politician became the chairman of the Railway Committee of the legislature and he used all of his considerable influence and power to ensure that policies were put in place that financed his railway.

In 1849, an act was passed in the Canadian parliament to provide

Sophia MacNab

Sir Allan MacNab's personal life was as turbulent as his political and business affairs. He outlived two wives and his only son was killed in a hunting accident while still a boy. His daughter, Sophia, was the delight of his life. While her mother was dying in 1846, Sophia kept a diary describing the routine of the family at Dundurn. The most touching entry was made on May 23 of that year.

I have not written in my journal for a fortnight and I hope Papa will not be displeased with me but allow me to leave out a fortnight and just merely say that poor dear Mamma was buried on Tuesday May 12 at two o'clock. There was an immense procession. They reached from here down to the grave. There were people from a great distance and also many women, black and white.

When MacNab was Prime Minister, Sophia went to Montreal, the capital, to be his official hostess. There, she met William Coutts Keppel Bury, the twenty-two-year-old heir to the Earl of Albemarle. The couple was married at Dundurn Castle on November 12, 1855, in a wedding that was the social occasion of the season. They later moved to England, where Sophia spent the rest of her life. Bury was active in British politics, elected to Parliament, and after he became a Viscount, went into the House of Lords. Sophia had ten children, but still had time to act as her husband's private secretary.

Many of the men who worked on it were poor Irish workmen who had recently arrived in the country. Troubles were not unknown. A resolution passed by the Municipal Council of Paris dated 1851 reads:

That a number of men are now employed in this neighbourhood upon the Great Western Railway and upon other roads here, and many of them are unruly and as the peace of this place is likely to be disturbed, application be made to the Government for the establishment of a Volunteer Rifle Company and that the Reeve do take such steps as may be necessary.[14]

Still, construction went ahead, and on January 17, 1854, the streets of Hamilton were alive for the most exciting event since the founding of the town: the coming of the railway. Main streets were decorated with bunting. At the intersection of King and James was a triumphal arch erected by the fire brigade. Finally, at 2 o'clock on the morning of June 18, the train arrived. Hamiltonians had been fortifying themselves in the taverns and bars all evening. When the wood-burning steam engine with its bulbous stack came into the Stuart Street station, pandemonium broke out.

Suddenly the clear icy air was shaken by an ear-splitting blast echoed by a hundred shouts: "The train from the Falls is in!" Contributing to the ensuing bedlam was the salute of the Rochester Brass Band which accompanied the American delegation and which now greeted the jubilant stationful of fanatics with the strains of "Yankee Doodle" and "Long Live the Queen." Complete strangers shook hands and slapped one another upon the back, offered drinks, or issued invitations to breakfast before the train pulled out for Detroit at six.

—Marjorie Freeman Campbell[15]

Great Western Railway Engine #51 crossing the bridge over the Niagara Gorge.

One person who was not at the celebrations was Sir Allan MacNab. He was at home with influenza. MacNab was often sick with gout and rheumatism in the latter part of his life. Despite this, in September 1854 he became Prime Minister of the United Canadas when the MacNab-Morin coalition was created. His government is best remembered for negotiating the Reciprocity Treaty that created free trade with the United States.

The irony is that MacNab, the fervent supporter of the British Empire, had entered into an agreement with Britain's old nemesis, the United States. In the end, he had become a railway man, and it was in the interests of the Great Western to have free trade. On May 21, 1856, MacNab was forced out of office by the supporters of John A. Macdonald. He died August 8, 1862, at Dundurn.

The Life of the Railroad Town

Hamilton was now a railroad town. It was the Canadian headquarters of the Great Western, where staff was responsible for the actual day-to-day operations. Another head office, which managed financial matters and policy, was located in London, England. Other branch lines feeding traffic into the main line were soon built. On December 3, 1855, a line was opened from Hamilton to Toronto, following the route that is still used today. It soon became the most profitable line of the railway. Additional lines were built to Guelph, Sarnia, Port Dover, and other centres.

One serious problem soon emerged for the railway. Legislation had been passed by the Canadian parliament, stipulating that the track gauge of all railways was to be 5'6" in width. The standard gauge used

The Crystal Palace, opened in 1860 in what is today Victoria Park, was a centre for exhibitions and cultural events. It was modeled after the Great Crystal Palace of London, and demolished in 1891.

on British railways and most American railways was 4' 8½". The reason for this decision was apparently that the British army was concerned about the threat of an American invasion of Canada. With the difference in the gauge size, the Americans could not use their trains on Canadian tracks.

But this decision proved to be a significant problem for the Great Western. One of the most compelling reasons to build the line was that the Ontario route was a shorter distance between New York and Chicago. But the difference in the gauge meant that rolling stock could not be used on both lines without the laborious and time-consuming task of adjusting the wheels. This proved to be impractical, and in the 1860s the regulation was changed and Canadian railways adopted the standard gauge.

Once the railway opened, Hamilton grew even more rapidly than it had in the past. Railway crews that worked up and down the line operated out of the city. In 1859, the Great Western Shops opened on Queen Street North, near the railway tracks. Here, 300 men built and repaired railway rolling stock of all kinds. The shops even built sleeping cars so that passengers could travel at night in comfort. At first, the iron rails used by the Great Western were imported from Britain, but they could not stand the Canadian frost. In 1863, a rolling mill was built in the shops and all rails for the company were rolled in Hamilton. Nearly the entire staff of the Great Western was British. Railway workers have always been a clannish bunch and the Hamilton men were little different. Almost all of them lived north of York Street between Queen and Dundurn, in an area adjacent to the railway yards.

But if the railway had a huge impact on Hamilton, it had an even greater impact on the rural areas it went through in southwestern Ontario. Now the farmers could market their produce and livestock and earn real cash. In addition, railroad engines could only get 36 miles to a cord of wood, so farmers could earn a good income by supplying fuel and at the same time clear their land for planting. Perhaps it is an exaggeration to call the coming of the railways a revolution, but to those who lived through that time it seemed a perfectly apt description.

The Desjardins Train Disaster

Little more than three years after the first train had come through the city, the Great

An artist's depiction of the Desjardins Canal train disaster of March 12, 1857, that killed 59 people.

Western experienced the worst disaster of its history. On Thursday afternoon, March 12, 1857, at 10 minutes past four, the Hamilton-bound train left Toronto. All was normal as the engine "Oxford" approached the bridge at Burlington Heights in the west end of the city. The train was moving at a speed of about six miles an hour and was on time in Hamilton for its 5:45 arrival.

As the engine crossed the new bridge, the front axle on the engine suddenly broke and the full weight of the engine came down on the bridge. The structure gave away with an awesome crash of splintering timbers. The engine gave a piercing shriek on its steam whistle, like

one last death cry, and plunged off the bridge into the deep chasm of the Desjardins Canal below, pulling the other cars along with it. The heavy engine crashed through the ice covering the canal, at a thickness of almost two feet. The baggage car turned on its roof as it plunged into the ice endwise and remained in that awesome position. The passenger car smashed though the 18-inch-thick ice, shattering glass and wood as it collapsed into rubble.

Fifty-nine people were killed in the accident and eighteen injured, among them some of the leading citizens of Hamilton. An overwrought *Spectator* reporter who rushed to the scene described it like this:

A national calamity may fairly be said to have befallen us. Men who have ever stood in the foremost rank — capitalists the most shrewd, speculators the most keen, merchants the most far-sighted, clergymen the most earnest — have at one fell swoop been taken from among us. The brain reels and the pen refuses to do its accustomed duty, when attempting to describe the heart-rending scene we have witnessed.[16]

Hamiltonians rushed to view the scene and help the survivors, but all that was left was the grim task of dragging for bodies in the waters of the canal and carrying the dead to the station house for them to be identified by the distraught families. A few days later, over 10,000 people in the city attended the funeral service for the dead.

The Water Works

Despite the unprecedented prosperity of the 1850s, disaster seemed to plague the city. In 1854, the same year the railway arrived in the city, typhoid fever, transported by the immigrant ships, struck.

Again the dead wagons creaked through the streets of the city, gathering the blackened corpses, many deposited outside their doors by the fear-crazed inmates within; again wound their slow way up York Street to the quicklimed burial pits.... Day after day, week after week as the heat mounted, as the flies multiplied and as the stench of sewage and garbage grew more overpowering, the pall of death deepened over the city.

—Marjorie Freeman Campbell[17]

To keep immigrants away from the city, all passengers arriving by steamboat were instructed to stay in sheds built along the waterfront, but most slept outdoors to avoid the dreadful conditions and contact with the sick. Doctors and medical staff worked in dangerous conditions for weeks as the epidemic raged. People grew short of food because farmers refused to come into the city with their produce. Finally, the epidemic ran its course, but not before 552 people died in the city. Hamilton was the worst hit of any centre in Canada.

The waterworks pump house and chimney opened in 1859. The building, largely unchanged since its opening, is now home to the Museum of Steam and Technology.

The big steam engines which pumped water out of Lake Ontario and distributed it to the city are still housed in the Museum of Steam and Technology. Steam was the major source of power in the late 19th century.

One of the conclusions of the epidemic was that the city had to improve its water supply and sewer system or risk the return of disease. There were numerous wells all over the city, but with the poor drainage and the use of outdoor privies, wells became contaminated. There was not even enough water to fight fires. The first city sewer system became a reality in 1855, and at the same time the city commissioned a study of the water system. After examining the problem, the well-known engineer Thomas Keefer proposed that the city draw its water from Lake Ontario.

This was an expensive undertaking, but City Council voted to follow Keefer's recommendations. A filtration basin was built near Van Wagner's Beach and a pumping station was built that still stands today on Woodward Avenue. The water was then pumped to a reservoir on the mountainside near Ottawa Street, and fed by gravity to the city. This project was a huge undertaking for a small city, and it came with a cost. An additional debenture of $774,412 was issued to pay for the waterworks.

To commemorate the project and advertise that Hamilton had an

Gore Park in 1860. The Gore Park fountain was built to celebrate the availability of clean, fresh water.

one-third of the buildings of the city were vacant and some areas were almost deserted. Writing in the *Spectator* on January 1, 1861, H.B. Wilson was very pessimistic about the future of the city.

The loss of 25% of our population, a decrease of 50% in rentals and a continuous 3 years of stagnation in all description of business, attended with the closing up of nearly all of our factories, were circumstances well calculated to dishearten the most hopeful and destroy belief in the prestige of our city.

—H.B. Wilson

abundance of fresh water, a fountain was built in Gore Park. It was first turned on July 4, 1859 and flowed for almost 100 years.

The Financial Crisis

The 1850s had been a time of great optimism but little common sense when it came to the city's finances. By the end of the decade, the people of the City of Hamilton found themselves in the worst financial crisis of their history. So much money had been borrowed to buy railway stock and construct the waterworks that over 75 per cent of the city's expenditure was going just to pay the interest on the debt. In 1858, over 25,000 people were living in the city, but once the true burden of the debt and the heavy taxation that would be required to free the city from that debt became known, people fled and the population fell to 19,000 by 1862. At one point, it was estimated that

Some of the creditors grew impatient with the slow payment of their debts and got judgments against the municipality. The sheriff sold the furniture in City Hall to meet the obligations, but the judgments were coming in faster than they could be satisfied. He was instructed to place a special assessment on the property tax, but that would have been impossible to collect and would have driven even more people out of the city.

It was at that moment that the city clerk, Thomas Beasley, the grandson of Richard Beasley, saved the day. He locked up the assessment rolls in a warehouse, hid the key, and then took a much needed rest in an unknown spot. His "cure" lasted until the court term for the special assessment had expired. He had saved the day, and in time the city was able to renegotiate its debentures, but for years Hamilton was crippled with debt. In 1864, fully 86 per cent of tax revenues serviced the debt, and by 1873 it was still 50 per cent. The situation looked desperate, but the condition of fear and pessimism would not last for long.

Chapter Four

The Manufacturing City
(1865 – 1890)

The Great Western enhanced the economic prospects of the city, but it did not make Hamilton the major centre of Canada West as some had hoped. Construction on the Grand Trunk Railway was completed a little after the Great Western. Its main line west of Montreal followed the north shore of Lake Ontario, through Toronto and Stratford to Sarnia, avoiding Hamilton altogether. The Grand Trunk became the principal railroad in Canada until the CPR was built in the 1880s. Hamilton merchants and financial institutions that had hoped to use the Great Western to capture trade found themselves in direct competition with companies from Toronto and even Montreal. They soon came to recognize that Hamilton would never become a major trading and financial centre. The city's future lay in manufacturing.

The Hamilton Policy

With the Reciprocity Treaty of 1854, Canadians had access to the American market. In the early 1860s, with the American Civil War raging to the south, farmers had a ready market for their produce, and with the railways they had an inexpensive way to deliver to that market. Horses, grain, cattle, and hogs all flowed south and much needed money flowed back into Canada. The Americans abrogated that treaty in 1866 because they were angry about the

The south side of King St., 1886.

British position on the Civil War and because they adopted a more protectionist economic policy with high tariffs. This created major problems for Canadians and, after 1873, with the onset of a deep economic depression, there were demands that Canada protect its own industries.

Hamilton industrialists were some of the major protectionist leaders in the country. Isaac Buchanan, MacNab's successor as Member of Parliament for Wentworth, headed an "Association for the Promotion of Native Manufacturers" which promoted a policy of high tariffs. He often raised the cry for protected markets at political rallies and in Parliament.

> *Free traders will say you pay more for the articles you manufacture than if you import them. Now I deny this is the case. Every article, I believe without exception, that we now manufacture, is furnished to the people at a lower price than it was sold before 1858.*
>
> —Isaac Buchanan[1]

Buchanan was so persuasive on this issue that John A. Macdonald called the campaign for high tariffs the "Hamilton Policy," but in 1879, when Macdonald adopted this as the policy for the government, it came to be called the National Policy. This policy of high tariffs was supported by workers and industrialists alike in the city. By the 1880s the city was booming. Expansion was everywhere and prosperity was on the rise.

The Birmingham of Canada

Hamilton became an important manufacturing centre for a number of reasons. Good transportation meant that raw materials could be easily imported and it gave access to markets. The city was close to the border and attracted American entrepreneurs and capital, the source of much innovation at that time. In addition, many of the city's immigrants brought skills with them from the rapidly developing industrial centres of Britain.

Shops along King St., 1865. W.E. Sanford started his ready-made clothing empire here. He became one of the city's wealthiest manufacturers of the late 19th century and was appointed to the Senate.

This early Hamilton manufacturer made popular toys.

Hamilton was also favoured by technology. In the early part of the nineteenth century, water power was used almost exclusively to drive mills. Ancaster, Dundas, and Waterdown had developed mills along their fast flowing streams, but steam power was more convenient. As early as 1864, steam engines were used in 43 per cent of the factories in Hamilton, and by 1880 steam power was virtually universal. Steam favoured Hamilton because the railway and ships could inexpensively transport wood and coal, the fuel used by the engines.

Metal fabrication was an early Hamilton industry. In 1835, John Fisher came to the city to produce threshing machines of his own design. He could not attract capital and invited a cousin, Dr. Calvin McQuesten, to invest in the company and join him as a partner. Fisher ultimately returned to the United States, but McQuesten settled in Hamilton. He bought the large stone house called Whitehearn that stands today and stayed active in the company with different partners until he sold his interests and retired in 1857. The company continued to operate well into the twentieth century, and the McQuesten family had a remarkable impact on Hamilton politics.

Stoves were another Hamilton product. In 1842, the brothers E. and C. Gurney, molders by trade, produced two stoves a day. By 1875, they were the largest stove manufacturers in Canada, employing 600 people in their foundry, which covered an entire block at John and Rebecca Streets. By 1890, Hamilton had become the leading stove manufacturing centre in the country.

Another leading industry was clothing. In 1862, William Sanford began manufacturing cheap, ready-to-wear clothes that combined style and durability. His company grew rapidly and produced shoes, boots, military uniforms, and other clothes. By the 1880s, Sanford employed over 2,000 workers in a big plant on King and John Streets,

Hamilton manufacturers in this era specialized in farm machinery.

Hamilton, Toronto and Buffalo were linked by telegraph in 1847. In 1878 Hamilton became the first city in Canada to establish a telephone exchange.

Dundas became an important textile centre with the establishment of the Dundas Cotton Mills in 1878. Within a year the company announced that it was "running to [its] fullest capacity in order to supply the demand."[2]

Richard Wanzer came to Hamilton from Buffalo in the late 1850s to found a sewing machine manufacturing company. By 1875, his factory, located on Barton Street, employed 800 workers and was producing 2,000 machines per week. Between 1861 and 1881 the company sold 1.5 million machines. In the 1880s, the demand for sewing machines waned. Wanzer attempted to diversify into coal oil lamps, but by 1892 he was bankrupt.

George Tuckett immigrated to Hamilton as a boy, in 1842. Tuckett first started manufacturing cigars in London, but returned to Hamilton in 1858 where he established a business at York and Bay Streets. During the American Civil War, his business boomed. In 1891, he opened a new plant at the corner of called the MacInnes Block, and by the turn of the century his clothing company was the largest in the country.

There were also important textile companies. The Hamilton Cotton Company on Mary Street manufactured cotton cloth, and

York and Queen Streets that was four stories high and had the most up-to-date equipment and facilities in the country.

It was a Hamiltonian who developed the first telephone exchange in the country. Hugh Cossart Baker, Jr., whose father had established the Canada Life Assurance Company, was a businessman with an abiding passion for the game of chess. He established a telegraph system to communicate moves with two chess mates. Then, in June of 1876, Baker attended a demonstration of the telephone in Philadelphia, invented by Alexander Graham Bell just two years previously. Baker immediately saw the application of the telephone system and a year later had hooked up a three-way telephone system with his chess partners so they could communicate their moves. By July 15, 1878, Baker had started his own telephone exchange with 10 telephones, the first in the British Empire, and by May 1879 had installed a long distance line to Dundas. Early in 1880 the name of the company was changed to The Hamilton Telephone Company, with 350 phones, and in that same year Baker got the charter for a Canada-wide company called The Bell Telephone Company of Canada. In December 1880 he sold his interests to Americans.

This period saw some readjustments. In 1882 the Great Western Railway amalgamated with the Grand Trunk, and in 1888 the Great Western shops, which had played such an important role in spurring industrial development in Hamilton, were dismantled and moved to Stratford, but this seemed to make little difference in the industrial development of the city. The 1881 census found 212 factories in the city employing thousands of workers. The city had reinvented itself as a manufacturing centre. "The Birmingham of Canada," it proudly called itself. Wealth and prosperity seemed assured.

Labour Begins to be Heard

The labour force expanded at a remarkable rate. In 1864, 2,300 workers were employed in the factories, out of a population of 19,000 people. By 1871, seven years later, the number of workers in Hamilton factories had increased by 52 per cent. Several of the manufacturers employed more than 200 workers. The 1881 census showed that out of a population of 36,500 people, 6,493 were employees; 4,935 of that total group were men, 1,027 women, 447 boys, and 87 girls. The males were concentrated in the higher paid industries like foundries, rolling mills, railways and sewing machine factories, while the females worked in the clothing industry, textiles and boot and shoe companies. It is a myth that women did not work outside the home in the nineteenth

By the 1890s, the core of Hamilton was completely developed. Because of the bay and the escarpment, the only room for expansion was to the east and west.

A middle-class ideal in the late 19th century was that women should not work outside the home. The reality was that most working-class women worked at least until they were married. Thousands laboured in Hamilton mills such as Tuckett Tobacco, shown here.

The other major divide among manual workers was between the skilled and unskilled. The skilled had better job security, higher wages, and greater prestige, but even they were subjected to a new, industrial style of discipline. Twelve- and fourteen-hour workdays, six days a week, was the norm. Wages for unskilled workers were at poverty levels. They had virtually no job security, and in times of economic downturn they were the first sent out the door. Even health conditions were poor. Workers who were injured were soon reduced to destitution. Tuberculosis was rampant and some jobs held special risks. Stonecutters, for example, rarely passed the age of 40 before they succumbed to lung disease.

Child labour was common. Most children were in the workforce by the age of 14, and it was not unusual for 9 and 10-year-olds to be working. They would be given special types of jobs, and were often called apprentices, even through this was usually an excuse to pay them low wages. In 1880, a group of 12-year-old boys who worked at the Wanzer Sewing Machine Company went on strike because their average wage of $3.82 a week was not enough to live on.

Early in the nineteenth century, Hamilton workers began to organize

century, but it is true that women tended to work in industries that paid lower wages than the men.

into unions and associations for mutual protection. The aims of that struggle were not only to improve wages and working conditions, but also to increase workers' control of their workplace. In those days, when any worker could be fired on the spot with no redress of grievance, and when there was a strong likelihood of being blacklisted for union activities, it took courage and fortitude for workers to challenge employers.

The first union activity in Hamilton and virtually in Canada was in 1833, when a group of printers went out on strike. They were helped by fellow printers from New York State, which suggests that some of them had come to Hamilton from the United States. In the 1840s building trade workers protested the use of convict labour. Over 500 men from the Great Western Railway yards went out on strike in 1856 because one of the men had been dismissed so that the foreman could hire a friend. The worker was rehired, but the workers' demand that the foreman be fired was rejected.

The 1860s mark the real beginnings of trade unions. Most were organized along craft lines. Some had links to British unions such as the Amalgamated Society of Carpenters and Joiners, brought over by immigrants. Others, such as the Typographical Workers (printers) and the molders, had links to unions in the United States. By 1864, a number of these craft unions had banded together to form a local Trades Assembly, the first of its kind in Canada.

A number of strikes took place during this period. Most were short tests of strength dealing with specific problems at the workplace, but some were long, involved struggles that demanded sacrifices. In February of 1866, the owners of the foundries in the city tried to break the control of the Molders' Union in their shops and tried to institute a blacklist against union men. The molders struck,

only to see scabs brought in from the United States. The struggle went on for months and was not settled until January 1867. By then, the union had lost the support of the workers and had disappeared.

In the 1870s and 1880s, the unions continued to grow and struggle for improvements. In 1874, the molders were again active. The owners, led by the Gurney brothers, locked out their workers in an attempt to drive down wages. This was a time of high unemployment, and the workers and their unions were in a weak position. The struggle went on for almost a year before it was settled. In March 1888, over 700 men in the building trades were locked out and the employers brought in scabs. By May, most of the men had returned to work.

Working Class Culture and Movements

By the 1870s and '80s a new industrial world had emerged in Hamilton. The city had become more polarized, between the upper classes who lived in big homes up close to the mountain, and the

In the late 19th century, Hamiltonians were becoming increasingly aware of the importance of education. The Hamilton Collegiate Institute and Normal School opened in September 1897. It burned to the ground in a spectacular fire in June of 1946.

workers who lived close to the factories and railroad yards in Corktown and north of King Street. There was also polarization in terms of income: the manufacturers became wealthy, skilled workers did reasonably well and many could even afford to buy houses, but there was also considerable poverty.

Unions were the centre of the social life of many of the working people in the city. Representing workers on the plant floor was only one of the union's activities. Most sponsored a number of gatherings every year for their members. Through the winter,

Tuckett Tobacco workers taking a break in 1891. The large number of children working at Tuckett was not unusual in this era.

each union would host a ball. Commemorative suppers were held, and in the summer there were parades and picnics.

On July 1, 1867, to commemorate Canadian Confederation, the city hosted a parade and the craft unions came out in force. The parade was headed by the "Friendly Brothers Union," a society of "coloured" men, followed by the fire companies, splendidly attired in their colourful uniforms. Then came the butchers, with an ox adorned with red and blue rosettes, the iron molders, the shoemakers, the bakers, and representatives of other trades.[3]

The procession was an important civic ritual in nineteenth century Hamilton. This is how Michael Katz, a historian who wrote about Hamilton life in the nineteenth century, describes it:

On every pretext work stopped and dignitaries, civic officials, representatives of societies, fire companies … all carrying their banners, marched through the thronged city streets to a public place where eminent men made speeches to rousing cheers. Often after the procession came a mass dinner and carousing at one of the local hotels, followed sometimes by a ball.[4]

When workers began promoting a broader political agenda, they naturally looked to the procession as a public demonstration of their support and solidarity. The struggle for a shorter working day was led by Hamilton workers. In the nineteenth century, the working day was 10 to 12 hours a day, six days a week, though 13-hour days were not unusual. Employers resisted the movement for a shorter workday. Finally, after considerable organization, Hamilton workers called for a march on May 15, 1872, a day billed as a "victory parade for the 9-hour day."

The procession included most workers in the city, shutting down almost

Tuckett was one of the leading tobacco manufacturers in Canada.

every workplace. Over 1,500 workers marched four abreast through the streets. Their banners announced, "Wisdom is better than Wealth." "On Time, Nine Hours," "United we stand, Divided we Fall." The blacksmiths carried a sign declaring "We strike the iron while it is hot." And the printers' sign proclaimed, "Art is long, life is short." The parade was the greatest display of the power of the union movement ever seen in the city. A poet wrote:

Honor the men of Hamilton,
The Nine-Hour Pioneers —
Their memory will be kept green
Throughout the coming years,
And every honest son of toil
That lives in freedom's light,
Shall bless the glorious day in May,
When might gave way to right.[5]

But despite their efforts, the gains of the Nine-Hour Pioneers were soon lost. Employers resisted and the depression of 1873 put workers on the defensive. Some employers, however, saw an advantage to a shorter workweek. George Tuckett was one of them.

We found that by starting in the summer time at 7 o'clock and working until 6, and giving them a half-holiday on Saturday, so that they could get off and enjoy themselves they worked steadier and with more vigor. In the wintertime we start at 7:30 and work until 6 o'clock. This allows the mothers to do the marketing in the daylight and we find that they can do the same amount of work in the nine hours, and then they appear more healthy and strong than when working the longer hours.

—George T. Tuckett[6]

In 1875, an assembly of the Knights of Labour was established in Hamilton, and by 1883, the Knights had six local assemblies with a combined membership of 880. The Knights mounted an idealistic movement that believed in co-operative ownership and production. They organized the skilled as well as unskilled workers, and advocated racial and gender equality, an unusual idea for the nineteenth century. Hamilton had the first so-called "coloured" lodges in the country, and the cotton and shoe factories of the city had a women's assembly.

John Peebles, a jeweller and later a Mayor of Hamilton, was a Knight.

I became a member of the Knights of Labour ... when I was quite a young chap. I thought its program would revolutionize the world, not only because of its program which included co-operation and state ownership of all public utilities ... and the purification of politics and of all law and state administration. (It) also included the full belief in the honesty and sincerity of all members of the order. In short it was a crusade for purity in life generally.[7]

Perhaps the greatest accomplishment of the Knights was their campaign for the free library movement funded by municipal taxes. But the movement of the Knights of Labour was short-lived. By 1885, it was in decline and by 1900, had virtually disappeared.

An old postcard showing the stairs up the escarpment at Queen St.

Associations, Sport, and Recreation

As Hamilton grew, a huge number of fraternal organizations, work related groups, sporting fraternities, and cultural associations developed. In this period, women were often isolated at home, caring for their large families, but men frequently joined groups to talk about work, promote their own interests or just have a good time.

In the 1850s and 1860s, volunteer firefighting occupied the time of many of the young men in the town. By 1857 the firefighters had 518 officers and men. There were four engine companies, a hose company, and a hook and ladder company. Every firefighter was given a uniform of a cap, belt, red shirt, light blue coat, white staff, and badge of office.

Company 1 was composed of young Orangemen, described as "a wild lot of boys." Company 2 started out with a strict temperance plan. No one was admitted unless known to be of strict temperance habits. The boys of Company 3 "were a convivial set and often indulged in crackers and beer, especially after a fire." These young men spent their free time hanging about the fire hall, polishing equipment, and chatting to their friends. No doubt many joined the firemen to participate in parades, and take part in the many oyster suppers and alcoholic refreshments that were all part of the rich texture of firehall life, but when the fire bell rang, the volunteers left their jobs, dropped everything, and raced to the scene. Sometimes they risked their lives.

This is an account of the burning of the Fisher and McQuesten Foundry:

Three members of #3 company were making a run for their lives through an alley between two of the burning buildings when one of the inside walls came tumbling down, covering them with a mass of stone and timbers…. Captain Shove ordered a roll call to discover the missing ones and their names. The alarm spread rapidly to almost every home in the city and anxious wives, fathers and mothers came rushing down to the scene fearing that it might be a son or a husband who had been killed…

All night long details from the several companies worked to remove the mass of stone and debris. When William Omand was reached, and he was still alive, what a shout of joy rang out on the air, and the anxious waiting crowd on the streets responded. (He) was tenderly lifted from under the mass of stone and carried out to the street when the doctors took charge of him. A short distance from where

The Aged Women's and Orphan's Home, photographed in the 1870s. The only support for the poor came from private charities and the municipality.

Omand was found were the bodies of his two comrades, pressed out of all form and shape.[8]

Accidents and illness were a constant concern. If the "bread winner" fell ill, the family was soon forced to rely on relatives or to receive help from church groups. Even worse, they could end up

A poster announcing a rifle shooting contest in 1876.

under the care of the House of Industry. Working people tried to protect themselves through self-help groups. The craft unions often had benevolent associations set up to play this role.

The Hamilton branch of the Foresters was founded in 1871, when 40 men assembled at Dan Black's Club House. The Foresters provided a type of insurance for working people against sickness and accidents by providing funds when a member was unable to work. The policy also provided a "widows' and orphans' fund," paid when a member died or was killed. Another benefit was that members could always count on a large turn out at their funeral, an important indication of the deceased's social status in the nineteenth century. The Foresters hosted suppers and dances, members had secret sayings and handshakes, and at meetings officers of the association paraded around with banners, axes, and spears that were symbols of the group.[9]

The intense conflict that marred relations between Protestants and Catholics in Toronto, New York, and Belfast was not as pronounced in Hamilton, but there were times when it broke into the open. On the night of August 6, 1878, a group from Toronto met some local men at the King Street rooms of the Emerald Association. After the visitors left by steamer, two Hamilton men, Dan

St. Paul's Presbyterian Church on James St. South, built in 1872.

Collins and Tom Brick, were confronted by a group of Orangemen in Gore Park. Soon, the True Blue Fife and Drum Band appeared along with 300 to 400 men all singing and marching around the Gore. Collins and Brick found themselves surrounded by a sea of unfriendly Protestant faces. They apparently gave a good account of themselves before the police arrived and restored order. The crowd was not so easily put off and headed for Brick's house in Corktown. Windows were smashed and Brick's wife, clutching an infant son to her breast, fled to a neighbour's house. Tom Brick seems to have survived with an enhanced reputation. He became prominent in a number of workingmen's associations and was a Hamilton Alderman for a number of years.

Baseball was the passion of the working men of the city. Teams were organized at various shops and factories. Craft unions were rarely without a team. Every evening throughout the summer the parks had after-work games between printers, cigar makers, molders, butchers, and other groups. Hotly contested matches took place between east-end and west-end teams. All of them attracted large crowds of relatives, workmates, and friends. People were drawn by the excitement of the game, a chance to meet with old friends and workmates, and the joy of a close match skillfully played. This is an account from the *Hamilton Evening Journal*:

The east end of the city presents a lively appearance every evening. All the avenues in the vicinity of the commons, as well as the commons themselves are occupied by baseball clubs…. It is understood that the shoemakers intend playing a match with the Hat Factory Club in a few weeks and no doubt it will be well contested.

In the fall of 1871, the Hamilton printers initiated what they called the "Great Typographical Base Ball Match" at the Maple Leaf grounds. Bauer's brewery transported large quantities of ice and beer to the park, "to quench the thirst of the large crowd anticipated." After the game, the printers retired to a local pub for a hearty meal and abundant liquid refreshment.[10]

The baseball game became the chief attraction of that other late nineteenth-century institution, the picnic. Companies, unions, churches, and almost every organization in the city had their picnics. During summer weekends, Oakland's, Dundurn Park, and the Crystal Palace Grounds would all be filled with many small picnics. Occasionally the city craft unions would organize gala picnics inviting skilled and unskilled workers from across the city. From 3,000 to 5,000 people would attend. Activities included games for children, speeches by the dignitaries and a huge feast inevitably organized by the women. The festivities culminated in a baseball game.

Few people were able to escape the city in the summer because they worked long hours, holidays were short and travel was expensive. Many went to the Beach Strip, but for most the bay and the escarpment were the source of recreation. Thousands of rowboats took to the harbour.

The Hamilton boats are built on the finest lines of the toughest and lightest timber. They are highly finished and thoroughly equipped with the best oars and are in every respect the finest lot of small boats to be found anywhere in the Dominion of Canada.[11]

An advertisement for an early Hamilton brewery.

There was no end to activities in Hamilton, and virtually all of them were organized by voluntary associations. Along with the sporting activities, there were amateur theatre, dance, and music groups, as well as literature and science associations.

Perhaps the most famous Hamiltonian of this era was a modest schoolteacher from Binbrook by the name of George Washington Johnson, who wrote the ballad, "When You and I were Young," in 1864. This sentimental song, which mentions an old mill thought to be Mount Albion Falls, was popular for decades.

The Militia

Another voluntary association that became important in the life of Hamilton was the militia. At this time, Canada had virtually no armed forces and relied on the British for military protection. When the American Civil War began in 1861, a number of Hamiltonians joined units of the U.S. Northern Army, but there were tensions between Britain and the United States around the war.

In response the British sent 18,000 regular troops to Canada. Five hundred members of the Prince Consort's Own Rifle Brigade were stationed in Hamilton for two years. They were billeted in the city and trained at the Crystal Palace grounds (Victoria Park). It was also decided to improve and expand the militia units of volunteers and a group in Hamilton formed the 13th Battalion in 1862. Three rifle companies, one of them a highland company, were also established. This is how Thomas Champion, who wrote an early history of the battalion, described them:

The companies … were fairly well drilled and ordered but their discipline was of the most rudimentary nature and they possessed more the character of military clubs than of efficient soldiers…. In those days the Canadian

After the American Civil War concluded, a group of Irish veterans living in the United States decided to further their cause of Irish independence by lashing out at Canada, a part of the British Empire. The Fenians, as the Irish nationalists were called, gathered in the Buffalo area and threatened to invade. The only military forces that Canada had at the time were the voluntary militia units. In April 1865, Hamilton's 13th Battalion was called up and sent to the frontier in the Fort Erie area. By September, the fear of invasion subsided and they were withdrawn, but in March of 1866 they were mobilized yet again. This is how Thomas Champion described the situation in the city:

British regular troops training on the grounds of the Crystal Palace in 1864. These troops were sent home after the American Civil War and were not available when the Fenians raided in 1866.

Militia was by no means a very popular force. It had not become fashionable then as it is now, and many people laughed and jeered at those, both officers and men.[12]

Hamilton at this time presented very much the appearance of being in a state of siege. A guard consisting of one officer, two non-commissioned officers and twenty-four men were in the drill sheds, a sergeant and a guard of twelve men were stationed at the artillery sheds and an officers' guard mounted daily at the Mountain View Hotel.[13]

Finally, in June 1866, the Fenians crossed the border. The 13th Battalion, under the leadership of Lieutenant Colonel Alfred Booker, met them at Ridgeway, along with other militia units. At first the Canadians gave a good account of themselves, and groups of Fenians were forced back into the woods, but then there were shouts that cavalry were about to attack.

"Prepare for cavalry!" Instantly the attacking party were formed into squares so as to meet the expected onslaught of the mounted force. The Fenians at once took advantage of the mistake and … poured a murderous fire upon them, whereby some were killed and more wounded.

—Thomas Champion[14]

Hamilton veterans who fought for the North in the American Civil War. This photo was taken during a reunion in 1887.

The horsemen never came. The Fenians fired on the exposed Canadians. Booker saw the error and tried to reform his column, but it was too much for the volunteers. They broke ranks and ran for shelter. Two members of the 13th were killed and several wounded in the engagement. The Fenians felt that they had scored an impressive victory, but their scouts told them that a large force of British regular troops were on the way to the battlefield. They soon retreated back across the border.

Booker was crushed by the outcome. He seems to have suffered a breakdown of some sort and he resigned from his position in the army. A court martial was held, inquiring into his conduct in the

The Battle of Ridgeway, artist unknown.

that they had to join together for mutual protection. This sense of urgency played an important role in the creation of Canada.

After the Battle of Ridgeway, the 13th Battalion became the pride of Hamilton. Isaac Buchanan, the city's leading politician and citizen, was the Commanding Officer. Annual balls given by the officers in the drill hall were popular events, and the regimental band was the pride of the city.

Life of the Rough

The militia, the manufacturing companies, the churches, unions, and working men's associations were all part of proper society, but as the city grew, a rougher side developed. On April 8, 1878 a *Spectator* reporter went to "drunk court." His report illustrates the moralistic journalism of the day.

Two drunks were elderly men who should have known better, while another pair was quite young, neither of them over twenty-three years of age yet, night

skirmish. He was completely exonerated in the inquiry, but it did little good. He was a broken man.

This incident would remain a minor footnote in Canadian history except for its political consequences. The Fenian Raids forced bickering politicians in the British North American colonies to realize

1888 Newspaper Stories

Temperance Meeting

Yesterday afternoon the Good Templar gospel temperance meeting was crowded to overflowing, many being unable to find seats. Edward Williams delivered an eloquent address on temperance, in the course of which he gave some excellent advice to the young men who were present.

—*The Spectator*, January 9, 1888

Runaway on King Street

Mr. Wm. Olmstead, an Ancaster farmer, was driving down James Street, near the corner of King, at about 9 o'clock Saturday morning, when his span of horses took fright and ran away. Mr. Olmstead held onto the lines and turned the horses up King Street. In front of the Bank of Hamilton the team took to the sidewalk, making a general scatteration of the pedestrians. In swinging around MacNab Street the wagon upset and Mr. Olmstead was thrown to the ground. He was painfully bruised, but not seriously hurt. The load of turnips were dumped in front of Mr. Bruce's seed store door. The horses escaped with a few scratches and the wagon was not much hurt.

—*Weekly Times*, April 12, 1888

A Pickpocket Captured

Mrs. Margaret Choate, residing at No. 30 Hughson Street South, was going through James Street market this morning when she felt a hand going into her pocket. It was not her own hand and therefore had no business in her pocket. She looked around and saw a young man quickly put his hand into his pocket. She accused him of stealing her purse, but he denied the charge. While they were talking Martin Daley was standing near. He saw the man throw a purse over his shoulder into a farmer's wagon and picking it up showed it to Mrs. Choate, who recognized it immediately as being hers. Constable Walsh came along and arrested the man.

—*Weekly Times*, April 12, 1888

Dropped From the Sky

C.W. Williams, of the firm of Williams & Young, aeronauts, performed a feat on Saturday afternoon that was never before attempted in this country. He dropped to the earth from a balloon with the aid of a parachute. The ascent was made from Dundurn Park. Owing to the heavy rain that fell nearly all day, and partly perhaps to a suspicion that the advertised event would turn out to be a fake, the attendance at the park was very small…. (But) it was no fake.

—*The Spectator*, June 4, 1888

after night they have sunk ambition and disgraced their manhood by asking for lodging in the cells and lying like dogs in a festering heap in a room reeking with foul smells and damned with the ghosts of dead hopes and the shadows of sin.

A sad case involved a young lad who was charged with sitting on the sidewalk blocking the passage of pedestrians. The boy was defended by his mother who, with a fluency and fervour, which only a mother can use when pleading for her flesh and blood, besought the magistrate to let him go.

The mother explained that her husband was cruel to the boy and would not let him stay in the house. She claimed that the boy gave her all the money he earned and she and his brothers and sisters would have gone hungry without those funds.

The mother wept, the son wept, the court was visibly affected — is it necessary to say the lad was dismissed?[15]

During the winter of 1864–65 the Parker Gang terrorized the city.

Joe Parker, alias Parish, was at the head of the gang and his headquarters was in a house on Market Street near MacNab where he lived with a brother-in-law named Taylor. A notorious gambler named Jim Jeffery acted as fence for the gang. He had a gambling establishment on the west side of MacNab Street near King.
The gang robbed several prominent wholesale

Postcard of the market.

houses until the proprietors were nearly ruined. Detective Armstrong located the gang and for some reason the arrest was entrusted to a posse of sheriff's officers who surrounded the house. Mister Parker cleaned out a window with a chair and placed himself therein with a revolver in each hand. He fired a fusillade, the bailiffs scattered and Mister Parker skipped over the adjacent fences and was seen no more.
Gambler Jimmy Jeffery was later arrested. In his house was an ingenious signaling system by which he could lean back against the wall as he sat playing at the table and a confederate in the room above, who was so placed that he could see his victim's cards, could signal to him.[16]

City Life

Hamilton was a walking city through most of the nineteenth century. The rich could afford to take their horse-drawn carriages downtown, or to their place of business, but most people had to walk. In 1873, Lyman Moore, a druggist, and his brother-in-law, Dr. Lewis Springer, obtained a charter to operate a public transit system. On May 11, 1874, the first horse-drawn cars, drawn along steel rails, came south from Stuart along James Street and turned east along King to Wellington. Soon, there was a second route in the southwest and another along York to Dundurn.

But public transit did little to change the character of the city. The downtown business core centred on Gore Park. There were two markets in the downtown. Close by were clustered butcher shops and grocery stores along with clothing stores, hardware establishments, and other stores. The downtown streets were alive with shoppers who walked into the central core to make their purchases. On market days, farmers came into the city with their families to sell their wares and to buy supplies, jamming the streets with a jumble of horses and carts and wagons. The city centre was noisy and dirty, but it was alive and vibrant.

This piece, written by an American journalist, appeared in the *Spectator*:

Today Hamilton has a population of not less than 50,000 and it has every appearance of being one of the most prosperous cities in Canada. It is now purely a manufacturing city and but little attention is given to commerce beyond the local demands of the citizens. Look down upon it from the mountaintop and it is one vast field of tall chimneys and smoke from its hundreds of factories hangs over the city like a beautiful web.

—*The Spectator,*
September 20, 1889

Immigrants aboard a ship in 1890.

Hamilton's first public transit system.

Hamilton had become a prosperous, thriving manufacturing centre, and in the process had become a leading city in the young Dominion. But as Hamilton grew and became more complex, the social fabric polarized along class lines. The wealthy and the middle class lived in a world separate from the labourers and craftsmen who worked in the factories. That polarization would soon have a great impact on the life and politics of the city.

Chapter Five

THE ELECTRIC CITY
(1890 – 1914)

Until the 1880s, the streets of downtown Hamilton were lit with gas lamps that gave off a dim glow which barely penetrated the murky shadows. When the first electric lights were installed on the streets, people were enraptured with the near-magical quality of the illumination. On warm summer evenings in the 1890s, the famous military band of the 13th Battalion played evening concerts in Gore Park and people flocked in the thousands to enjoy the music and marvel at the twinkling lights strung in the trees. It seemed like progress was bringing unimagined wonders and opportunities to the city.

Hamilton's Second Industrial Revolution

The dying days of the nineteenth century and the first decade and a half of the twentieth brought a second industrial revolution to Hamilton that was every bit as profound as the changes wrought by the railways and the National Policy. This revolution not only changed the way people earned their living and brought faster growth than ever before or since, but also changed the city ethnically and religiously so that by the eve of the First World War Hamilton was a place of remarkable cultural diversity. Two key economic

developments spurred this revolution: electricity and steel.

By 1890, Hamilton was already a manufacturing city with a concentration of companies in the iron and steel industry, but none

Twinkling electric lights brought a magic to Gore Park in the 1890s.

of them produced their own iron or steel. In 1893, a group of New York financiers decided to build a primary steel making facility somewhere in Ontario to take advantage of the protected Canadian market. The City of Hamilton offered free land, cash bonuses, and tax concessions if the company had a blast furnace and open-hearth facility up and running by 1894. The land was a local beauty spot on the harbour (which was then outside the city limits) called Huckleberry Point, the present site of the enormous Stelco plant.

At first, the Hamilton Blast Furnace Company had serious problems. The original group of investors fell under suspicion for financial malpractice and was bought out by a new group from Hamilton led by William Southam, of the *Spectator*, Senator Alexander Wood, a wholesale hardware merchant, and John Milne, a foundryman. The brick smokestack that was under construction blew down in a gale, delaying the project for several months, but on December 31, 1895, 500 city residents were taken by train to the new facility to witness "the blowing in of the furnace." Now the city was a primary producer of steel as well as the centre for the fabrication of a host of steel products.

An equally important development for Hamilton in the 1890s was the development of electric power. Electric lights were rapidly gaining in popularity, and in 1892 the Hamilton Street Railway built a steam powerhouse on the bay to produce electricity for its streetcars. The day of the horse-drawn trams was over. But the

A 1903 souvenir magazine promoting the city. The images show the steel mills, and the canal on the beach strip.

industrial applications of electricity promised the greatest benefits.

John Patterson, a local businessman, built a steam-generating electric power station on Victoria Avenue, but he dreamed of a more economical means of generating power. He joined with four other men, John Gibson (later Sir John Gibson), a prominent Liberal provincial politician, lawyer, and businessman, John Moodie, John Dickenson, and John Sutherland. They came to be known collectively as the "Five Johns." This group set up the Cataract Power Company to generate electric power at DeCew Falls, near St. Catharines, and transmit it 32 miles to Hamilton.

Up until this time, no one had been able to transmit electric power this distance, and there were many who were skeptical that it could ever be done. The group gambled on a new idea called "alternating current." They built immense transmission towers from their generating plant to Hamilton and when they turned on the current they found that it transmitted brilliantly. A practical way had been developed to transmit power long distances and Hamilton basked in the achievement by renaming itself "The Electric City."

An advertisement for Hamilton's cheap electricity.

Major factories, such as International Harvester and the steel companies, were established along the waterfront in the east end of the city in this period, prior to the First World War.

These two accomplishments, a primary steel making facility and inexpensive electric power, were both completed by 1898, and they contributed to unprecedented economic growth. Existing Hamilton plants rapidly converted to electric power because it proved less expensive, and many new steel fabrication companies came to the city to be close to the steel mills.

American branch plants were attracted to Hamilton. Westinghouse came in 1898. Its plant at Barton and Wentworth was the company's first manufacturing operation outside of the United States. The Deering Harvester Company bought a huge property beside the Hamilton Blast Furnace Company in 1902 and built a plant to manufacture agricultural implements. Their enormous

The foundry department of Westinghouse in 1905.

Barnes Carriage Company in 1906, Berlin Machine Works in 1908, Standard Underground Cable in 1911, and Proctor and Gamble in 1915. All of these firms and others settled in the east end of the city, and most located their plants along the waterfront.

The steel industry continued to boom and to change. In 1910, the Steel Company of Canada, later renamed Stelco, was formed out of a number of other metal producers in Ontario and Quebec, including the Hamilton Blast Furnace Company. After the merger, a decision was made by the company to concentrate steel production in their facility at Huckleberry Point. In 1912, the Dominion Steel Castings Company was formed. It later came to be called Dominion Steel Foundry Company, or Dofasco. Other Canadian companies settled in the east end: Brown-Boggs relocated to the Sherman and Barton area in 1913. Hamilton Bridge Works

manufacturing facility on the waterfront became the largest farm implement factory in the British Empire. Otis Elevator came in 1902, American Can Company in 1904, Union Drawn Steel in 1905,

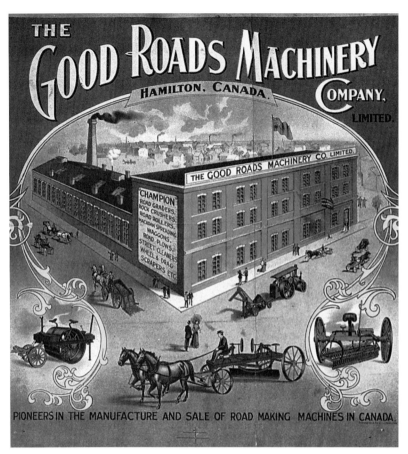

A Hamilton-based equipment manufacturing company.

relocated to the Depew and Beach Road area, Frost Wire Fence came to Hamilton in 1904 and National Steel Car was founded in 1912.

With this massive investment in the east end of the city, workers flocked into Hamilton and the population soared. In 1890, there were 44,653 people living in the city, by 1900 the numbers climbed to 51,561, by 1910 the population jumped to 70,221, and by 1914 it leapt again to 100,808 people. The city almost doubled in size in the first 14 years of the twentieth century.

The New Worker

The industries of Hamilton in the nineteenth century had been dependent on skilled craftsmen. The iron molders, the printers, the carpenters, and the shoemakers all dominated their crafts and the places where they worked. Production was impossible without their skill and supervision. But in the last two decades of the century, many of the skills that had been the monopoly of the craftsmen were engineered into machines. The work was simplified and sped up. By the turn of the century, the nature of manufacturing had changed to such an extent that skilled workers were often eliminated altogether. Machines were doing the work, and in new plants, such as the ones in the east end of Hamilton, semi-skilled workers were hired to tend the machines.

Canada's immigration policy, after the Laurier government came to power in 1896, was to encourage the "stalwart peasant" by favouring agricultural workers from eastern and southern Europe who

Members of the Barton St. Methodist Church evangelize on the street in 1910. The Methodists were leading advocates of the prohibition of alcohol.

factories that were springing up around the country.

The unskilled immigrant worker had one basic commodity to exchange—his physical strength, his brute force, to carry, to pull, push, turn, as a horse would do, or a piston or a wheel. He exchanged it from sector to sector as the demand for human machines shifted to a rhythm he could not but obey.[1]

The majority of the immigrants in this period were still from Britain. They quickly integrated into Canadian life, but the so-called "foreign workers"—anyone who was not Anglo-Saxon—were given the hottest, dirtiest, most strenuous and poorest paid jobs. These ethnic workers streamed into Hamilton to take the unskilled jobs in the new plants that opened in the east end of the city. A *Globe and Mail* reporter visited the city in 1913 and reported that:

There is unfortunately another element that is inseparable from industrialism—the men who do the coarse work that is necessary in large industries. The average English-speaking immigrant will not take up this work. It must be done, however, and the men from northern, southern and central Europe are called upon to do the cheaper class of work—to serve as it were, as hewers of wood and carriers of water.

—*The Globe and Mail*, March 1, 1913

The Dofasco foundry in 1914.

were expected to homestead in the Canadian west. Many of these immigrants, perhaps even most, did not have the resources or experience to be farmers. A large number took work on the many construction projects that were going ahead at that time or in the new

The working conditions that these workers faced were primitive, and there was almost no concern about their safety or well-being. Often companies would not even record the names of their "foreign" workers, and on some occasions workers were killed on the job and their families were never notified. Many of these workers were men who had come to Canada alone. Their object was to earn money to send home to their families or to save enough to bring their families to Canada. They lived in ethnic ghettos centred around Sherman and Barton Streets, and crowded into houses, sometimes sleeping in shifts. Some even lived in shacks within the property of companies.

Not only was prejudice directed against the "foreign element," but so was considerable fear. The *Hamilton Herald*, a newspaper that had more sympathy than most, described the census takers of 1911, who ventured into the "jungles of the foreign district," as having the "courage and persistence of a Livingston or a Stanley." The census takers reported that some houses they visited had plaster coming down from the ceiling and one found a seven room house that held twenty-eight members of a family, plus boarders.

The condition of practically all the houses was more or less deplorable, though in some a surprising degree of neatness was evident even when there were many dwellers therein. Taking all in all the

A postcard showing tenement houses in downtown Hamilton. The tower in the background is City Hall.

section was not by a wide margin as bad as similar districts in other cities.
—*Hamilton Herald,* June 28, 1911

On March 1, 1913, *The Globe and Mail* commented that:

These ("foreign" workers) congregate in colonies, principally in the northeastern part of the city, and retain, to a large extent, their native customs and habits. One of the worst of these is love of strong drink. Their rallying point is often a beer keg or a whiskey bottle, with the common result that quarrels arise and frequently knives are used freely, sometimes with fatal effect.

Little evidence exists that the non-Anglo-Saxon group had a higher crime rate than any other group, but there was much talk of Italian "Black Hand Societies," and demands for prohibition were strengthened because it was seen as a way to impose "Canadian ideals of citizenship on the foreign element."

Newspapers of the day tended to call everyone "foreigners" who did not have English as their first language, but each group had a different history and experience. The largest group was the Italians. They first started coming into Hamilton in the 1890s to work as construction labourers on the Toronto, Hamilton and Buffalo (TH&B) Railway. It is estimated that there were about 5,000 Italians living in the city by the First World War,

International Harvester brought a number of Poles from their plant in Chicago to work in Hamilton. More joined them, and their community grew in the Barton, Sherman area. Like the Italians, the Poles worked hard to build their church, St. Stanislaus, as the centre of life for their growing community.

Jews were living in Hamilton as early as the 1850s, when Herman Levy opened a jewellery business. By 1853, a handful of German Jews banded together to organize the Hebrew Benevolent Society, Anshe Shalom, but like other groups the first wave of heavy Jewish immigration came in the period prior to the First World War. Many of these people fled pogroms in Eastern Europe and arrived in the city impoverished. Efforts to help them were made by Jews and non-Jews alike. Their community at this time tended to gather in the northwest end of the city around Queen and York Streets.

The Sicilian town of Racalmuto, the original home of many in Hamilton's Italian community.

but it is difficult to say with any accuracy because all of the ethnic groups were underestimated by the census. A contingent came over from the Sicilian town of Racalmuto, and many more were to come to Hamilton from this town in subsequent years. In 1910, the community was established enough to have an Italian chapel at St. Ann's School on Sherman Avenue, and by 1912 it had a church called St. Anthony's.

Numbers of the children had their first experience of Canadian life at Hess Street Public School.

Other groups also came in this period. The Hungarians, Ukrainians, Armenians, Yugoslavians, Russians, Lebanese, Chinese, and others who continue to live in the city can all trace their origins in Hamilton to this time prior to the First World War.

Stanislaus Kostka Roman Catholic Church on Barton St. East.

Labour and the Street Railway Strike

The trade union movement was poorly prepared for the new industrial world that emerged in this period. Skilled workers were threatened by the changes brought by industrial production. They saw their "monopoly of skills" being eroded, and reacted in a defensive way by turning to their craft unions for protection not only from their employers but also from the unskilled who they believed were taking their jobs.

The treasurer's ribbon from the 1887 Labour Day Parade.

There was talk of industrial unions, where all the workers of an industrial plant would be members of the same union, regardless of skill. Certain unions, like the Industrial Workers of the World (the IWW or Wobblies as they were called), advocated this type of structure. The Wobblies were active in both Canada and the United States, but did not gain many supporters in Hamilton because most skilled workers strongly opposed them.

In the first decade of the twentieth century, the city emerged as a stronghold of craft unions. The only Canadian organizer of the American Federation of Labor, the central organization of craft unions, was John A. Flett, a Hamilton carpenter. By 1903, Hamilton had 59 labour organizations, including broomworkers, furniture woodworkers, lathers, iron molders, bicycle workers, and others.[2] Virtually all of them had connections with international (American) unions. Many of these unions were militant in the defence of their members. There were strikes, boycotts, sympathy strikes and other actions, but they represented only a small number of workers, and the

Hamilton Steel and Iron Company workers in 1910.

vast and growing number of unskilled workers were not involved. Sometimes workers who were not allowed into their organizations scornfully called these craft unions "the aristocrats of labour."

Hamilton employers, like others across North America at this time, took a very aggressive stance with their workers. They knew the unions were weak, and they had an abundance of cheap unskilled labour that they could shape in directions they wanted. Employers looked for ways to speed up the pace of work, and if workers gave even a hint of trouble, they were soon sent packing.

Despite the unprecedented boom of the period, workers' standard of living did not improve. The hours of work gradually decreased, but wages increased only gradually until about 1905, when they stabilized until the outbreak of the war. Even some of the craftsmen found that

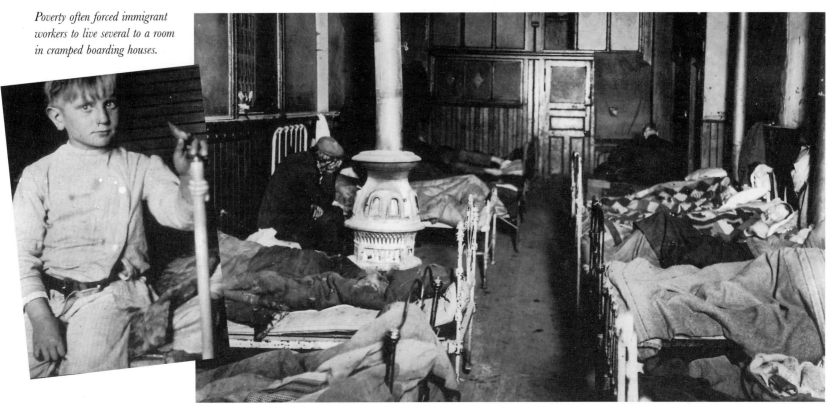

Poverty often forced immigrant workers to live several to a room in cramped boarding houses.

their unions could not help them. After 1909, the demand for stoves collapsed and most of the iron molders, whose union had been one of the strongest in the city, found themselves out of work. But there was one action during this time that reflects the latent militancy and feelings of frustration of workers. This was the Hamilton Street Railway strike of 1906, the most violent strike in the city's history.

The 180 drivers of the HSR went on strike on Sunday November 4 for increased wages and the recognition of their union. The workers had a lot of sympathy in the city because the Cataract Power, Light and Traction Company, which owned and operated the street railway, had become very unpopular. Many ordinary Hamiltonians believed that the company charged exorbitant fares

and provided poor service. The strikers had strong community support, and when the company chose to import strikebreakers from Buffalo to continue running the trams in defiance of the strikers, many were outraged.

Within days of the start of the strike, the situation deteriorated. The union distributed "we walk" buttons and thousands of people wore them, indicating their support for the strikers. In the evenings, thousands gathered on the downtown streets. As streetcars, driven by scabs, came along the tracks, there were threatening protests. The demonstrations escalated every night. Rocks were hurled through the windows of the trams. Passengers huddled on the floors of the cars as glass shattered about them. Windows in the building owned by the

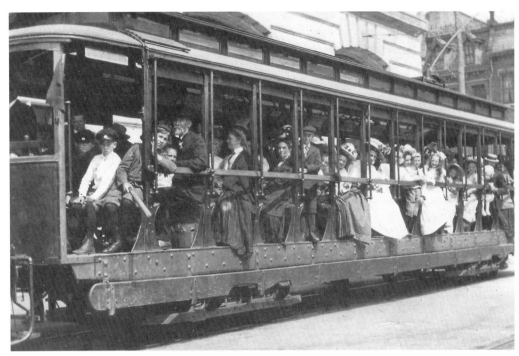

Hamiltonians heading out of the city for a day in the country in an open radial car, about 1900.

Mayor Biggar was sympathetic to the strikers, but the mounting disorder in the streets and the demands by various elements of the population to do something about the anarchy were too much for him. He appealed for calm but was ignored. The Chief of Police told him that the police were unable to maintain order and protect property. The newspapers predicted more violence. Mayor Biggar finally asked the military for help.

Militia units from Toronto were sent in and cavalry arrived from London by train. During the evening of the tenth day of the strike some 15,000 strike supporters milled about in the downtown. The military took up positions around City Hall to the jeers of the crowd. The army carried Lee Enfield rifles and the cavalry pulled out their sabres. Stones were thrown by members of the crowd. Mayor Biggar advanced, raised his hand, and asked for order, but his voice was drowned out by the shouts of the mob. Then he ordered Sheriff Middleton to read the riot act. As

company were broken and the offices ransacked. Policemen who attempted to stop the damage were beaten up. Rumours spread that the rowdy foreign element was plotting devious acts and violence was taking over the streets of the city. This is how the *Hamilton Times* described the situation on November 23, 1906:

> *Never before in Hamilton's history has control of the city been so completely lost to the police or the central district been the scene of such wild excitement and rioting as followed the Street Railway Company's first attempt to operate its cars after dark. From a crowd that numbered a few hundred at 7 o'clock, there grew a howling mob that numbered fully 15,000.*

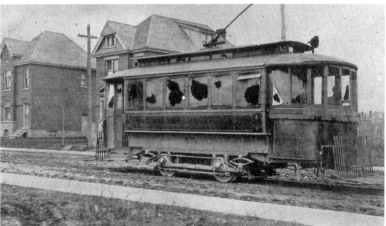

A streetcar smashed in the 1906 Hamilton Street Railway strike.

An early Hamilton police vehicle.

the Sheriff concluded with "God Save the King," the order was given and the military attacked the crowd.

As the militia charged, their officer shouted, "Give it to them, men! Give it to them!" This is how a newspaper reporter described what happened.

> *Behind the police came the dragoons, belaboring citizens about head and shoulders with the flats of their swords. They pranced their horses along the sidewalks with a great clatter of hooves. The infantry brought up the rear, using their rifle butts on laggards and on the argumentative.*
> —*The Spectator*, November 25, 1906

Over 200 people were injured, 50 of them seriously. Protesters were chased into buildings and beaten. Ben Kerr, a piano player in a restaurant, was clubbed as he played for the patrons; Jones Lewis, on his way to work at the *Hamilton Herald*, was pursued even into the

editorial offices; a patient leaving Dr. Roseburgh's, at King and Hunter, suffered a broken head and was soon back for medical attention; police Constables Hallisey and Bleakley were seriously injured by bricks; Hans Hansen, on his way to work, was felled by a blow, and when he got up was knocked down again; Charles Dodsworth, on his way to play at the Grand Theatre, was chased for blocks and then injured.3 The military battled the crowd for four hours but finally, after midnight, the violence began to subside.

The next morning, there were accusations and recriminations. Citizens complained to Mayor Biggar that the military had overreacted, but Colonel Denison, the head of the military operation, was most satisfied with the actions of his men and described it all as an exhilarating adventure. The strike was ultimately resolved. The workers' union gained recognition but did not win a wage increase. But this violent repression of workers' rights would shape the politics of Hamilton for many years to come.

Conservative, Liberal, and the ILP

Up until this time, Hamilton was dominated politically by middle-aged men prominent in business or legal circles. Women in Ontario did not even have the vote. Some opportunities existed for working men to hold office municipally, but none of them were able to use those positions as stepping-stones to political office in senior levels of government.

Labour leaders in the city had long spoken out against this political monopoly. In the 1883 provincial election, the Knights of Labour ran their own candidate, Edward Williams, a locomotive engineer. *Labor Union*, the Knights' newspaper, urged Hamilton workers to vote for "one of their own number" rather than men of "influence, wealth and organization."

Different dates could be selected for Hamilton's centennial, but not 1913.

It has long been felt as a grievance by the wage earning class that their interests have been too long overlooked in legislation. The cause of this neglect is obvious. Every other considerable class had its representatives on the floor of Parliament. Lawyers, physicians, merchants, farmers, bankers and lumbermen were all represented. Every class and interest could voice directly and at first hand its claims and grievances. Labor alone had no spokesman.

—*Labor Union*, February 17, 1883

Sir John Gibson and his house on Ravenscliffe Drive. The house, which is still a private residence, was recently restored.

Allan Studholme was an English immigrant who settled in the Hamilton area in 1870. He learned his trade as a stove mounter (an assembler of cast iron stoves) at the E. and C. Gurney Company. In the 1880s, his activity with the Knights of Labour got him blacklisted with employers, but he never wavered from his objective of making labour's voice heard in political circles. He was a small man with intense eyes. Later in life, Studholme sported a salt and pepper beard and white hair, which gave him a distinguished look, but it was his sterling honesty, compassion, and straightforward no-nonsense style that attracted working people to him. By 1906, his prominence won him a seat on the Board of Arbitration of the 1906 Hamilton Street Railway strike. That very same autumn, when the member of legislature for Hamilton East died, Studholme ran for election as a labour candidate and won a convincing victory.

The street railway strike undoubtedly played an important part in the victory, but it also reflects a shift in the politics of many Hamilton workers. By the first decade of the century, the mood of workers was decidedly more radical. Demands were made for industrial unions; political "soap boxing" outside plant gates and in working class neighbourhoods like James Street North and the Sherman/Barton area was common; a Marxist political group had taken an office across the street from the city hall and published a socialist paper called *Cotton's Weekly*, dedicated to fighting "the battle of the plain people." Studholme represented a more conservative wing of this labour political movement, but the "little stove mounter," as he called himself, was an influential political figure in his own right.

Labour's supporters in Hamilton were determined to capitalize on the victory. After the election, the Independent Labour Party (ILP) was formed and became the political vehicle to help Allan Studholme win the next three elections. The ILP grew in members and organizational talent. It ran candidates for local elections and won seats on the city council. As Labour's only member in the provincial legislature until 1919, Studholme sat as an independent, far on the back benches, struggling to make his voice heard. Over and over again, he championed measures to improve working conditions, safety precautions, and workers' compensation. Often he stood in the legislature to speak out against the flooding of the labour market through government-assisted immigration. He did not challenge the right of capitalists to "own the means of production," as Marxists were doing, but he constantly attacked land speculators and utilities magnates.

The most controversial and important issue that Studholme supported was women's suffrage. Every year between 1910 and 1914 he introduced a bill in the legislature to grant women the rights to vote and hold public office. The first year it failed because he could not get a seconder to the motion. The next year, with the gallery packed with suffragettes, he said in the debate, "With their splendid intelligence and magnificent education [women] … [are] just as capable as any man sitting in the legislature."[4] Studholme was still in the legislature in 1917, when the Ontario legislature finally gave women the vote.

Students of a home economics course in 1910.

A New Role for Women

Dr. Elizabeth Bagshaw

Prior to the First World War, women were becoming much more prominent in a variety of fields. More and more were working outside the home in factories and other fields. International Harvester even employed women in jobs that were usually reserved for men. More women were graduating from Central Collegiate, which opened in 1896, and some went on to university. Elementary school teaching had become an occupation that was almost an exclusive preserve of women. There were even professional women, such as Dr. Elizabeth Bagshaw, who practised in the city.

Social welfare had long been considered a special interest of middle and upper class women, and Adelaide Hoodless, the wife of a prominent Hamilton businessman, became an internationally known figure for her efforts to gain better training for women in homemaking skills. She had lost a child as a result of contaminated milk. This tragedy led to her campaign for the formation of Women's Institutes for the instruction of "scientific household management," in 1893. The first Institute was established in Stoney Creek in 1897 and soon the movement spread around the world.

At first, the efforts of Hoodless were derided. The *Spectator* editorialized: "Are Hamilton mothers no longer able to teach their daughters how to cook?"[5] But she fought back and soon had her male critics on the defensive. By the time she died in 1910, at the young age of 53, she had been involved in the formation of a number of organizations such as the National Council of Women and the Victorian Order of Nurses.

A hand-tinted lantern slide showing women shoppers in the Hamilton Market in 1911.

A City Divided

By 1900, Hamilton was a city polarized along class lines. The new industrial might created wealth at a phenomenal rate for those who owned and managed the factories. This was a time before income tax, capital gains tax, or inheritance taxes, and the families that were in that small circle of the wealthy lived with an opulence that has never been equalled. The neighbourhood of the upper class was in the southwest of the city, and many of their magnificent houses on gracious tree-lined streets that were built at this time can be seen even to this day.

The workers, on the other hand, lived close to the factories in the east end of the city or crammed into the older neighbourhoods of the North End and Corktown. As they struggled to make a living, many of the unskilled labourers lived in poverty in the ethnic ghettos that had developed. Others, however, found

These well-preserved houses in the neighbourhood around Barton and Mary streets were originally built as workers' homes.

The Tuckett mansion on the corner of Queen and King streets, is now used as the Scottish Rite.

new opportunities. Vacant land was inexpensive, and neighbourhoods close to the factories developed to house the thousands of workers who were streaming into the city in search of work.

Brightside, the neighbourhood north of Burlington Street, immediately to the west of the new Deering Works (International Harvester) and the Hamilton Steel and Iron Company (Stelco), was born in 1905. Lots cost between $150 and $200, and could be bought for as little as $5 down and $5 a month, but even that was too expensive for some. Most who settled in Brightside were Italians, but there were also Poles, Ukrainians, and others. An advertisement by the developer read:

It is our intension to endeavor to dispose of the lots to a desirable class of workingmen and thereby assist to make Brightside a pleasant district in which to reside and at the same time add value to the property.[6]

The area south of Barton Street and east of Gage Avenue was developed as the factories moved east. Factory owners who were eager to recruit a dependable work force developed some of the early neighbourhoods. Other areas, like Union Park between Ottawa Street and Kenilworth Avenue, were developed by real estate speculators. The better paid skilled workers employed in the factories could afford these houses. The frame, one-storey and one-and-a-half storey homes that still line these streets were often built by the owners in their spare time after work. They developed intense pride of ownership.

Incline Railway, Head of James Street, Hamilton, Canada.

The mountain was a huge barrier to development until the James Street incline railway opened in 1890. The incline operated until 1931. A second incline was built at Wentworth Street in 1900. It closed in 1936.

Many of the thousands of skilled artisans who are employed in [Hamilton] factories own their homes. Modest many of them are, but they indicate comfort and, having a stake in the community, their occupants are continually making improvement in the buildings and their surroundings. This is particularly noticeable in the summer time when row upon row of well-kept buildings display small gardens or grass plots. In and about these may be seen the working men trimming and cutting in the evenings after their day's work, or on Saturday afternoons when nearly all the factories are closed. These constitute the great class of Hamilton.

—*The Globe and Mail*, March 1, 1913

The other neighbourhood that began to develop before the First World War was the mountain. There had always been a few people living along Concession Street. A toll road gave access up John Street from early in the nineteenth century, and in 1873, James Jolley built the Jolley Cut with his own money. He donated his road to the city on the condition that there be no tolls. However, in that day of horses, the 300-foot rise of the mountain was a difficult obstacle. Then, in 1892 the James Street incline railway was built, and in 1899 another incline was built at Wentworth Street. Each incline had two cars that counterbalanced the weight. They could take wagons, horses, bicycles

Boys on Barton Street in the city's North End.

and 30 to 40 passengers who sat in an enclosure. The price was two cents for adults and one cent for children. With the inclines travel to the mountain was suddenly remarkably easy. After the turn of the century the mountain experienced its first real building boom. Summer homes that had been built by city people to gain the cool mountain breezes were winterized, Concession Street grew into a business centre, and Upper James acquired stores, schools, and churches.

One of the strongest neighbourhoods in Hamilton was the North End, that patch of the city north of the railway tracks and west of Wellington Street. This is a reminiscence of Alf Ready, a man who grew up there and later became a union leader in the city:

In the North End in those days the bay was clean and beautiful. Kids learned to swim, fish and play on the ice before they even went to school. I learned to sail and swim by the time I was five. There was a place called the Baby Hole where all the kids used to swim without bathing suits. Girls and all, it didn't matter. We used to jump off the boathouses and roofs. It was a great place. The fishing was tremendous. The best. Every kid could catch a basket of perch like nothing, and a few bass and the odd pike.

There was a great bobsled run on Mary Street that ran about four blocks right down to Ferrie Street…. The

people used to get out there at night with great big washtubs full of water and flood the hill. Holy Hanna, twelve o'clock at night, and they would finish flooding the hill and come down—some of those bobsleds would hold ten or twelve people.[7]

The Radials

Hamilton was a city on the move. Railway service was still good, and in December 1895 the first train of the TH&B Railway came through the city. John Moodie bought the first automobile in 1898. This is his description of what it was like to venture out on the roads:

The Beamsville radial car allowed people to commute into Hamilton from outlying towns, and allowed farmers throughout the region to bring their produce to market.

The Hunter Street tunnel for the Toronto, Hamilton & Buffalo Railway was dug in the 1890s. INSET: The Bascule Bridge over the canal on the beach strip.

In those days if you ran twenty-five miles without a puncture you considered yourself lucky. The roads were vile, the tires only a faint suggestion of what tires were to become, and we were always picking up horseshoe nails.[8]

But it was the radials that gave people a new mobility. In the 1890s, the electric age brought electrified trams that rode on rails to destinations well beyond the city limits. The Cataract Power, Light

The clubhouse of the Royal Hamilton Yacht Club on the canal at the beach strip. Hamilton's upper crust came here to dance, take moonlight cruises, and socialize. On Sept. 18, 1915, this building was destroyed by fire.

and Traction Company came to own four lines that radiated out from the Terminal Building in downtown Hamilton. One went to Dundas, another line was laid east through Stoney Creek, Winona, and Grimsby, to Beamsville, a third through Ancaster to Brantford and the longest went through the suburbs and factories of the east end, across the Beach Strip to Oakville.

With the radials people could get out of the city with ease and visit places like the Royal Hamilton Yacht Club, the hotels and amusement park that were built on the Beach Strip, or the orchards and small towns on the Niagara Peninsula. The radials gave access into the city for farm people and those who lived in surrounding villages and towns. Radials even encouraged the first wave of commuters who worked in Hamilton but lived beyond the city limits. A trip on the radials brought a sense of excitement and change to everyone who rode on them.

The men with their flowing moustaches, and the young blades decked out in fancy striped jackets, sailor straw hats or derbies, was a sight long to be remembered. The teenaged girls donned their best ankle length dresses, starched shirt-waists, feather or flower-trimmed hats with a bird or two perched on top. The homeward ride, usually at night, was an exhilarating experience as these old cars gathered speed through the open country, lurching from side to side as they sped down the rails.[9]

The radials made the beach strip easily accessible, and Hamiltonians began to flock there in the 1890s. In 1903, a popular amusement park opened on the beach strip. There were boathouses and slides, and in 1912 a Ferris wheel was erected.

Teens enjoying themselves on the beach strip.

Theatre, Vaudeville, and Moving Pictures

As the city grew, people had a little more time, and entertainment of various sorts blossomed. Hamilton had always been a centre for theatre. The Garrick Club, an amateur theatre group, put on presentations from 1875 to 1910. There were elaborate professional theatrical presentations at the Grand Opera House and productions at Bennett's Theatre and the Savoy. One of the most successful was Summer's Mountain Theatre, which opened in 1902. A favourite outing was to go up the incline railway to the mountain brow to enjoy

The Hamilton Garrick Club, a popular amateur theatrical group, was formed in 1875. The club continued until 1910.

one of the productions. Summer's Theatre burned down in a spectacular fire on December 21, 1914.

There were a number of popular entertainment events and spectacles. Travelling circuses came to town. In 1897, Buffalo Bill brought his Wild West show and played to capacity audiences at the circus grounds near Wentworth and Barton. Vaudeville was particularly popular in Hamilton, and the city was on a regular circuit of travelling performers. One of the advantages of vaudeville was that immigrants did not need a good command of English in order to enjoy the show.

Moving picture shows became all the rage about the turn of the century. There were a number of small theatres in Hamilton that offered one-reel silent melodramas and comedies, usually accompanied by a piano player, for five cents (thus the name "nickelodeons"). The Royal, on King Street West, offered a two-hour show of six reels for ten cents. But the new movies proved to be controversial. In 1907, School Trustee Charles Booker put forward a motion at a board meeting condemning the films with strongest disapproval as:

Places of amusement where immoral suggestive pictures are displayed.... Four of the five pictures which I looked at were of such a low, degrading nature that I would blush with shame were I to try and amuse my children by letting them look at them.[10]

The Hamilton Tigers football team of 1904.

Miss Tiger, a pinup girl in the 1890s.

The Sporting Life

By the 1890s, Hamilton had become a sports city, with some of the best athletes in the country and fans that packed each match to cheer on the local team. Hamilton teams were called the "Tigers," and yellow and black were the colours as early as 1872. Those were the days of amateur sport, when players had to take time off work for games and pay their own expenses. They often had to bring their own lunch when they went out of town, but there was a pride in wearing the Hamilton colours. Athletes felt they were competing for the glory of their town and team as well as for personal recognition.

Football was first a sport of the middle class, but by the turn of the century some of the best players were boys out of the North End and Corktown. Hamilton played exhibition games against the University of Toronto, Harvard, and Chicago teams. By the 1890s, the enthusiasm for the game led to the organization of the Ontario Union League and Interprovincial Leagues. In 1910, Ben Simpson led the Tigers into the Grey Cup against the University of Toronto at a game played before 12,000 people, the largest crowd for an athletic match in the city up until that time. When the Tigers lost, the crowd rioted. In 1912, another Hamilton team, the "Alerts," won the city's first Grey Cup and the Tigers repeated it the next year.

The bicycle craze of the 1890s captured the imagination of many Hamiltonians.

Hamilton girls have not yet taken kindly to the abbreviated skirt and, as a result, the bloomer does not appear in view unless there is a tumble.

—*The Spectator,*
May 8, 1896

Hamiltonians seemed to participate in every activity that was popular in the day. There was sailing and rowing on the bay in the summer, and ice fishing and ice boating in the winter. Lacrosse remained popular. In 1893, the Jockey Club constructed a racetrack at Ottawa and Barton Streets.

By the 1890s the city was in the grip of the bicycle craze, and despite their long skirts women took to the sport with enthusiasm.

The past week has been an ideal one for cyclists and the appearance of King and James streets every evening has been wonderfully enlivened by the devotees of the health-giving sport. One of the things that has surprised the weary pedestrians who have watched the never-ending procession of wheelers night after night is the large number of women riders. They do not all show themselves in the glare of day but at night they come out in full force, spinning up and down the asphalt. Curious ones have been waiting patiently for the sight of the bloomer girl.

Hockey and baseball teams competed against other centres, but if there was one sport which athletes from the city excelled at, and gained international recognition in, it was long distance running.

In 1894, the *Hamilton Herald* newspaper established the Around the Bay Race, which attracted world-class marathoners. Today it is considered the oldest race of its kind in North America. A number of Hamilton runners soon were excelling in the long distance race, but the city also produced world-class sprinters. By the turn of the century, a whole group of runners participated in the sport and a number of clubs supported them.

The Around the Bay Race was first run in 1894 and attracted runners from across North America. The great Mohawk runner, Tom Longboat, is number 26 in this 1908 photo.

Friendly competition developed between a number of local runners, including John Caffery and Billy Sherring from Hamilton, and Tom Longboat, from the Six Nations Reserve, who were members of running clubs in the city. Caffery and Sherring had both won the Around the Bay Race when they set their sights on the Boston Marathon, the premier long distance run in North America. In the 1900 race, Caffery placed first and Sherring second, astounding the Americans. When they returned home, the *Spectator* declared them the "gallant runners from the northern zone."

Caffery became sick and dropped out of competition for a time, but Billy Sherring continued to win races. In 1906, the first Olympics of the modern era was to be held in Athens, Greece, and Sherring was determined to compete in it. His problem was that he did not have any money. Billy was a railway porter. He earned a modest wage and paid all of his own expenses out of his own pocket. Greece was halfway across the world. How was he going to get there? He

managed to save $75 out of his wages. The St. Patrick's Athletic Club, which he ran for, added another $90, but this was not nearly enough. As it happened, a friend of his trained horses and all the money that Billy and the club had saved was put down on a horse named "Cicely." When it placed first, Billy had the money he needed.

Sherring travelled to Greece in steerage and arrived a month early. He trained and even worked a little to get some money to live on. The night before the race, he slept on a hard, wooden floor in the town of Marathon where the race was to start, along with plenty of "livestock," (bed bugs) while athletes from other countries were housed in luxury. The day of the race was sweltering, but Billy had a plan, and he set about executing it with the discipline that characterized everything in his life. He wore a big floppy hat to shade him from the blistering sun; on his shirt was the Irish shamrock, symbol of the St. Patrick's Athletic Club; and in his hand he carried a maple leaf flag, symbol of his country.

Billy Sherring winning the 1906 Athens Olympic marathon. On his left is the Greek Crown Prince.

runners. Billy would occasionally walk to preserve his strength, but as the race went on he became stronger and stronger. He passed the American Bill Frank at about the three-quarter mark and then came within sight of the leader, the Swedish runner Svanberg. His pace steadily increased until he passed the Swede. After that, he slowed down a little until he saw Svanberg gaining on him. With characteristic grit, Billy broke into a run, eating up the miles until he was a long way ahead.

As he approached the stadium in Athens, cannons boomed out to announce that the marathon runners were approaching. Billy ran into the stadium to the momentous cheers of 140,000 spectators. He had to run one

The steamship Modjeska coming through the beach strip canal.

As the race started, the field of runners sprinted off and Billy hung back at the end of the pack, letting the others set the pace, waiting for the time to make his move. The heat exhausted all of the runners, Billy included, but he conserved his strength. By a quarter-way through the gruelling 26-mile race, he began to pass other

Bobby Kerr winning the 220-yard sprint at the 1908 Olympics in London, England. INSET: *Bobby Kerr.*

lap around the track to complete the race, and as he ran the circuit the excited Greek Crown Prince, dressed in naval uniform, ran with him. Billy crossed the finish line well ahead of any of the other competitors and set a world record of 2 hours and 51 minutes.

Billy Sherring was honoured by the King of Greece and was awarded a five-foot high bronze statue of the goddess Minerva, along with a goat. When he arrived back at the city of his birth, Hamiltonians welcomed him with an outpouring of joy and pride. As the steamship *Modjeska* pulled into the dock at James Street North, just blocks away from where he was born and grew up, the wharves were thronged with people. A mob of 40,000 people lined the streets holding torches as Billy rode from the harbour to the city hall. There, a huge celebration was held, with speeches by Mayor S.D. Biggar, the same mayor who had ordered the militia's attack on the crowds in the Hamilton Street Railway strike.

There were other world-class Hamilton runners in this era. Bobby Kerr won the 220 sprint in the 1908 Olympics held in London, England, and came to be called "the greatest sprinter in the world," but it was the small railway porter, Billy Sherring, who first made the world recognize that Hamilton and Canada had athletes in the top ranks of the world.

Hamiltonians felt a great pride in the accomplishments of their athletes. With the dramatic growth in industry and the increase in population, it appeared inevitable to many that the city would soon be the leading centre in Ontario and even Canada. All things seemed to point to a rosy future for Hamilton. Little did the people of the city know of the trials that lay just ahead.

Chapter Six

WAR AND AN UNEASY PEACE
(1914 – 1940)

Many remembered the period before the First World War as a time of innocent pleasures when people were happy, progress seemed assured, and troubles in the world were distant and unimportant. There is some truth in this vision for members of the middle and upper classes in Hamilton. Workers, on the other hand, particularly the "foreign born" workers who laboured in the big factories and construction sites of the city, faced poverty and constant hard physical work. What these filtered memories reflect is not the innocence of that age but the contrast between that period and the grim reality of war in the trenches.

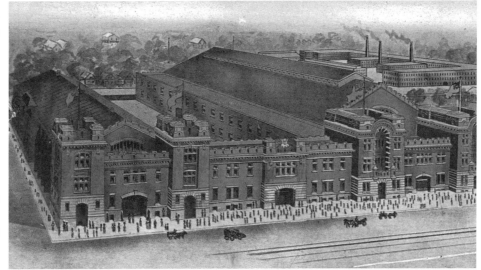

A colourized postcard showing the Hamilton Armouries, where recruits departed for the First World War.

Volunteering for "The Great War"

In the summer of 1914, people in Hamilton, like people all across the country, grew increasingly excited by events in Europe. Special editions of the newspapers of the city, detailing the threats and ultimatums of the major powers, were quickly sold out. Canada was part of the British Empire. When Germany invaded Belgium and the British Foreign Secretary, Sir Edward Grey, demanded that they withdraw, Canadians knew that these decisions would determine their fate. The Germans refused. The British ultimatum expired at midnight, August 4, 1914. Canada was at war.

Some saw the future with prophetic clarity:

The lamps are going out all over Europe; we shall not see them lit again in our lifetime.
> —Sir Edward Grey, British Foreign Secretary

But in Hamilton, the declaration of war led to frenzied excitement and unbridled patriotism.

Hamilton has never witnessed such scenes as took place in the city streets last night and probably never will again…. The streets were packed with an enthusiastic crowd of excited men and women whose customary serenity and calmness of manner had completely deserted them and in its place had arisen the true spirit of imperial devotion—the spirit which, at times of war has always permeated the breasts of the citizens of the British Empire whenever the Empire was in danger….
Magnificent is the only word, which fittingly describes the proceedings at the armories last night. The drill hall was packed with men and women. The former had come to respond to the call from the government offices at Ottawa to volunteer their services for the fighting line in Europe and their womenfolk's mission was to cheer them on and encourage them in their self-sacrificing enthusiasm for the cause of empire. And how they cheered. The band of the 91st Highlanders … formed a square in the rear end of the hall and played successively "Rule Britannia," "Oh Canada," "The Maple Leaf" and "God Save the King" and at the conclusion of each rendering hats were flying high in

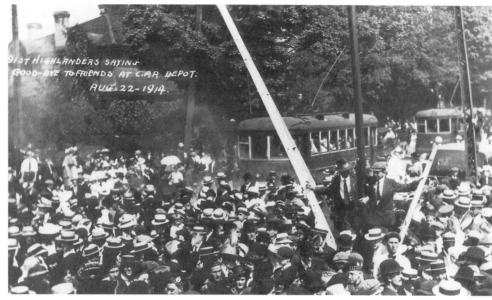

Well-wishers saying goodbye to recruits in August, 1914.

the air and the great building resounded again and again with the joyous, excited shouts and cheers of men and women. This was no lukewarm enthusiasm either. It was straight from the hearts of these people and it was eloquent testimony of the strength, their union and their common devotion to the national imperial cause. If there was one circumstance, which gave rise to the feeling of discontent, it was the inability of the men to at once rush to the scene of the war.
> —*The Spectator*, August 8, 1914

Hamiltonians had already established a long military tradition. Since the 13th Battalion had fought at the Battle of Ridgeway, the men had trained and socialized together in their spare time. Their military band was among the best in Canada and they had won numerous rifle marksmanship awards. During the Boer War (1899–1902) the 13th Battalion had contributed a strong contingent to the 7,000 Canadians who volunteered. Shortly after the turn of the

Life in the trenches during the "Great War."

first Hamilton recruits for the Great War were chosen.

Everyone who followed these matters predicted that the war would be over by Christmas. If Canadians did not hurry they would miss the whole show. The government had asked for 20,000 volunteers, and men from across the country scrambled and begged to be given the opportunity to serve. So many Canadians wanted to join that 33,000 men signed up, exceeding the quota by 13,000.

The first group to go to the training camp at Valcartier, Quebec were the volunteers for the Princess Patricia's Canadian Light Infantry, a group that were almost all veterans of the Boer War. On a sultry August evening, they marched to the train station, wearing civilian clothes with their medals dangling from their chests, through the crowded streets, echoing with the cheers of the excited population. On August 22, the main infantry group entrained for Valcartier, and then a Field Battery left on August 28, and each time the streets were lined with cheering people. Then, on August 28, news came of Hamilton's first casualty. Private Joshua Gee, fighting with the British Expeditionary Force, was killed in the retreat from Mons.

The Home Front

Once the first wave of volunteers marched off, the military authorities of the town became concerned that the thousands of immigrant workers living in the city, originally from countries that were now enemies, might engage in sabotage.

We have several thousand foreigners to look after here and with a hard winter and feeling running high it is hard to tell what might happen unless there is a strong force to maintain order.

Charles W. Heming, Scout Commissioner
—*The Spectator*, November 14, 1914

Allan Studholme supported the right of women to vote.

century, a second regiment, The Argyll and Sutherland Highlanders, was formed in the city, and by 1914 enlistments in the two regiments was at an all-time high. It was from these two militia groups that the

Quickly a home guard force of 1,000 men was posted at various points in the city such as reservoirs, pump houses, and bridges. "No loitering is to be permitted on the part of citizens," ordered Scout Commissioner Heming, and the guards were ordered to fire upon anyone caught in damage of any kind. Some thought this was rather silly until it was reported that a bomb had been set off at Dominion Foundries.

The excitement soon settled, and boredom set in with the home guard. On September 20, 1914, the Hamilton volunteers left Canada with the First Contingent to Europe. Since 1913, a serious economic depression had left many of the big factories idle and large numbers unemployed. With the first flush of the war it was expected that Hamilton industry would soon be working at full production, but nothing much happened until well into 1915. By then the character of the war was becoming apparent.

This was no war of glory and dashing heroes, such as the ones described in the boy's almanacs that were popular at the time. It was a war of attrition in which armies were caught in the mud of trench warfare and each side pounded at the other with deadly artillery and cut down enemy attackers by machine gun fire with industrial efficiency. Canadians were in the front lines from March 1915 to the end of the war, and from the first day the lists of casualties flowed back to the home front with frightening regularity. Every day until the end of the war Hamilton newspapers recorded the names, ranks and units of local men killed or wounded at the front.

By the middle of 1915, recruiting had become increasingly difficult. When the volunteers marched through the streets to the railway station, the crowds were not cheering. Mothers cried, wives and girlfriends clung desperately to their men at the train station, and children knew that this could well be the last time that they saw their

Recruiting booth in Gore Park during First World War.

fathers. And yet, reluctantly, men still joined the war effort.

The Hamilton Recruiting League became a fixture in the city. The League set up a display and held rallies in Gore Park in front of Queen Victoria's statue, where prominent citizens like the Mayor, Allan Studholme, and many others tried to shame men into joining the army. "Are Mothers Obstructionist?" asked one appeal. A recruiting officer harangued the crowd, pleading with the men to join up. When none came forward, he heaped scorn on them: "Not a move! Then you must be admitting you are cowards. You are not British!"[1]

Many women spent every spare moment on war-related volunteer work. Campaigns were waged to "knit for the war effort." Men who were felt to be shirking their duty were presented with white feathers. Marion Crerar, president of the Hamilton Branch of the Imperial

The 205th "Tigers" Battalion was set up to recruit athletes, and Bobby Kerr, the great runner, became their adjutant. (The Tigers Football Club lost 25 players and former players in the war.) In the 1917 election, the people of the city elected a full slate of Union candidates who promised to bring in conscription, but even when it was enacted it could not satisfy the war machine's demand for men.

As the casualties mounted, the wounded returned to the city in increasing numbers. They were admired, but their injuries often made them unemployable.

Recruiters used every method possible to get men to sign up, from calls to patriotism to accusations of cowardice.

An 86th Machine Gun Battalion soldier said that one employment agent told him that "returned

Order of the Daughters of the Empire (IODE), worked unstintingly for the Recruiting League. Three of her sons had gone to war, and she saw the conflict as a type of holy war.

Do you know that, as I sat at church service today, it came to me, as it had not before, that God is surely with us. Do you know that the crosses of our flag are the crosses of St. George, St. Andrew and St. David? And do you know that the emblem of the tyrant is the double eagle—a carrion, a bird of prey? And that the crest on the helmets of his military are Death's heads and cross bones. Young men, you are wanted. Won't you go?[2]

As the war dragged on, other recruiting methods were used.

soldiers were most unsatisfactory, that they had nothing but hard work to offer and that they had enough cripples of their own to look after." To this the soldier replied: "Were I fit for hard work I would still be in uniform not applying for work here." S.L. Landers said: "We promised these soldiers so much when they enlisted. We said 'boys go!' We pledged ourselves to look after them upon their return from the front and it is up to us to live up to our pledges."

—The Spectator, November 8, 1916

Maj-Gen Mewburn was the Union Government candidate for Hamilton East in the 1917 federal election.

By the fall of 1915, the war orders began to come into the large factories, and by early 1916 a serious shortage of labour had developed. In February, women began to be hired in the steel mills and other heavy industry in jobs that had always been considered men's work. But the full employment did not lead to higher wages. Inflation rapidly eroded living standards so that by war's end the real income of workers had dropped significantly. Meanwhile, the profits of companies engaged in war production soared. Soon, there were accusations of war profiteering.

Shell production in the Bertram Foundry during the First World War.

Not only did the euphoria that had marked the early days of the war vanish, but a sense of bitterness set in. The "returned men" felt particularly isolated. Few could understand their experiences in the trenches other than their comrades in arms. The wounds of many were so serious that they were incapacitated. They had seen their friends die under horrible conditions, and many had difficulties coming to terms with their experiences.

Hamilton had contributed more than any other centre in the

Recruits marching to war through the Hamilton streets.

country. People of the city had donated over $4.5 million to the war effort. Fully 10,000 men from the city had volunteered, the highest rate of enlistment of any centre in the country, 2,000 were killed and it is estimated that up to 7,000 had come home wounded. By the end of the war, the mood of optimism and belief in progress had vanished.

Labour Breakthrough

The intense period of labour unrest that emerged right after the First World War in part reflects the disillusionment of returned soldiers, but it had more to do with the erosion of living standards as a result of inflation. By 1919, just as the returning soldiers resumed civilian life, unemployment began to soar. In the winter of 1921–22 it

The period following the First World War was a time of intense labour radicalism. Craft unions were the dominant force in the labour movement at this time.

reached 15 per cent in the city. In 1919, protests arose across Canada, culminating in the Winnipeg General Strike, and in Hamilton, many steelworkers and other groups had their first experience with craft unions.

An Ontario provincial election was called for in October 1919, and much of the frustration of people across the province was channeled into this event. The old-line parties, Liberal and Conservative, were challenged by two new groups: the United Farmers of Ontario, formed in 1914, which expressed the political and social discontent in rural areas and small towns, and the Independent Labour Party. During the war, the ILP was organized in several centres across the province, and in the 1919 election they ran a number of candidates in different cities.

In Hamilton, the election was one of the hottest ever fought. The ILP ran candidates in all three ridings in the city. Walter Rollo, a broommaker and president of the party, ran in Hamilton West, on the slogan of, "Your vote for Rollo is a nail in the coffin of the profiteer." George Halcrow, a plumber recently elected a City Controller, ran in Hamilton East, and Will Crockett, a Labour-Farm candidate ran in Wentworth. Much of the action was fought out at political meetings on the streets and at the plant gates at shift changes. This account of a meeting gives something of the flavour of the campaign:

Six men described as "Socialists" went to a street meeting of an independent labour candidate Lieutenant Sam Landers. When he was about finished his speech Fred Flatman, one of the socialists, challenged Landers by saying that he had with him a man who would prove him a crook. The candidate made a spirited defense.

"I have known this man Isaac Shapiro for 20 years and have fought him in labour matters many times during that period. He is a rabid socialist as you are Fred Flatman and you Lockart Gorden and that big Russian you have with you. You aren't going to make this a meeting to promote Socialist propaganda because I refuse to allow it. If you want to talk Socialism hire a wagon or get a soapbox for yourselves, but you cannot come here and work that game. Friends we'll close this meeting in the old British way by singing the national anthem and take off our hats as we sing it. Our Socialist friends here boast that they do not sing the national anthem or take their hats off while it is being sung."

Lieutenant Landers must have known this would stir up a storm. "I protest against the singing of the national anthem!" shouted Lockhart Gorden.

John Hendrie was a wealthy industrialist who was also a prominent politician at the turn of the century.

James St. looking north in 1925. In the background is the old city hall with its clock tower. As the congestion in this photograph shows, increasing numbers of people had private cars.

"I don't care a rap for your objection. We'll sing it and take off our hats as we do."

—*New Democracy,*
October 16, 1919

According to the account, then the "pep" got into the meeting and it got very hot for the stalwart six. They were set upon by the big crowd, and their hats were torn from their heads. Lockhart Gorden held onto his with both hands and pulled it down over his ears, but he had a lively time of it. The gathering dispersed after giving three cheers for the Soldier-Labour candidate.

Spirited meetings like this took place all over the city during this election. When the votes

Horse-drawn delivery carts were a common sight as late as the 1950s.

Ice fishing on Hamilton Bay finally stopped in the 1920s because of concern about pollution.

were counted, the Independent Labour Party had won all three Hamilton seats. They joined in coalition with the United Farmers to form the government and, overnight, Walter Rallo went from broommaker to Minister of Labour, becoming the first working man in Ontario to hold a cabinet position.

The Farm/Labour government introduced a number of progressive pieces of legislation. They extended the school-leaving age to sixteen, passed a minimum wage bill, and legislated hours of work, but the coalition was bedevilled by fundamental splits. The Farmers wanted a reciprocity treaty with the United States, to reduce the tariff on farm machinery, while Labour supported high tariffs. The Ontario Temperance Act, which legislated prohibition, had strong support from the Farmers and was opposed by Labour. By the end of their term, the government began to dissolve as a result of dissent and defections.

During their term, the Farm/Labour government was faced with serious social problems. Unemployment was high, and cities were responsible for relief but had few resources to draw on in dealing with the problems. The hardships of many people, particularly the returned soldiers, were severe. This account appeared in the *Spectator*:

The Hamilton Market, where various produce was sold, was the centre of Hamilton life for decades.

Through the depression that lasted until 1923, a series of demonstrations kept the city in turmoil. On January 7, 1921 a meeting of the unemployed took place in Market Square. Several hundred people showed up to hear the speeches and demands for action. To a cheering crowd, Edgar Haslem shouted, "Have you left your courage in France? Let's go out and get what we want!" "Where's the ammunition?" someone replied. The crowd marched to City Hall, others joining on the way. Someone pounded on the door, demanding to see the mayor, but when they found that he was not there they marched off to his house on Queen Street. It was only when Mayor Coppley promised to help the unemployed that they dispersed.[3]

A few weeks later, four members of the Unemployed Association were charged with sedition arising out of this protest demonstration. In the jury trial in April, evidence was given that these men had made radical statements and had Bolshevik

Wounded and incapacitated ex-service men were compelled to reside with their families in tents on the eastern limits of the city and their suffering during the recent heavy rains had been pitiable. Soldiers were unable to pay the high rents demanded and were being driven out of their homes.

—The Spectator, July 20, 1920

literature in their homes. Mayor Coppley testified that he had been called a "profiteer." But the jury refused to convict the men. When the verdict was read, people in the courtroom broke into loud applause.[4]

The May Day march in 1922 ended in a confrontation that was described by the *Spectator* as a "general riot." At 2:30 p.m., 1,200 demonstrators reached King and James Streets. The traffic officer grabbed the red flag that was being carried and was immediately attacked.

The reserve squad (of police) were called into action with drawn batons and it took but a few minutes to disperse the crowd…. After the leaders and women were taken into custody the (group) reassembled on the market square where torrid speeches were made.

—*The Spectator*, May 1, 1922

These demonstrations were dismissed by most in Hamilton as the work of a small group of radicals, but they reflect the frustration that many workers felt. Labour had been able to gain some degree of political power, but their disappointment in the Farm/Labour government had left them feeling that all their efforts made no difference. By 1923, employers were in the ascendancy. Technologies were being introduced in the plants to speed up the work, increasing numbers of workers were paid by piece rates set by the "time study man," and employers advocated the open shop in which workers were not required to join unions. Even the trade union movement itself held to the craft union model that did not have a place for the huge number of unskilled industrial workers who laboured in the big mills of the city. By 1923, the number of unionized workers had decreased dramatically from its high in 1919. The people of Ontario and Hamilton turned away from the Farm/Labour government when prosperity returned, and elected the Conservatives.

Woman selling honey at the Hamilton Market in the 1920s.

Fashion, Work, and the "Fairer" Sex

The crisis produced by the First World War created more social change than any comparable period in the twentieth century, and those changes affected women even more than men. For example, for 100 years, modesty in women's fashion was an unbending rule. Women wore dresses and skirts down to the ground and grew their hair long. Then, during the war, hemlines began to rise. First they were mid-calf, then at the knee, and then even above the knee. Women cut their hair in the new "bobbed" style. Many older people were scandalized by what they saw as frivolous fashions. They predicted that these outrageous styles would not last and demanded that everything return to "normal."

In April 1920, Miss M.J. Urry, president of a Hamilton business women's club, contacted the *Spectator* to complain about the sorry state of affairs. She had some very severe strictures to make on what she termed the "nakedness of numerous georgette clad girls with not enough underclothes on to cover themselves decently."

Women's fashions in the 1920s reflected the "new look" of the independent woman.

And the pity of it is that they do not feel embarrassed in the least. I do not know what girls are thinking of. Thinking people in the presence of such bad taste in

Catalogue showing women's fashion in 1930.

public places are really mortified. Girls ought to uphold the standard of things. It's up to them to help men run straight. You don't have to be a nun. You may have a wonderful time in the world but the moment you leave modesty out of your life then your troubles begin. I believe it is principally the younger girls who need a helpful suggestion, though I do know some married people who need a little jacking up. We are going to take up the matter at the next meeting of the club and there will probably be a resolution scoring the present indecency.

—Miss M.J. Urry, *The Spectator*, April 19, 1920

Despite Miss Urry and the resolution of the women's club, fashion did not change. Women, particularly young women, were enjoying a level of freedom and independence that they had never experienced before. They scorned the "fuddy-duddies," as they called them, adopted the new fashions, and bobbed their hair. Dancing crazes swept North America. The tango, Charleston, and black bottom were all the rage in Hamilton. Young people flocked to the new dance halls like the Winter Garden and the Royal Connaught Hotel.

Jobs were opening up for women, though most of them were still in traditional areas of "women's work." Even in January 1920, a time of high unemployment for men, the *Spectator* and the other papers were filled with ads for women: "Office girls wanted," "good general servant," "lady typist," "Women to scrub factory floors," "Housekeeper," "Girls wanted in Mercury Mills. Work pleasant and

working conditions healthy. Experienced girls can earn higher wages and any bright girl willing to learn has no difficulty in rapidly learning work that pays well."[5]

Young working women were viewed with some suspicion because they violated the middle class notion that girls should stay at home until they were married. A survey in 1920 found that 13 per cent of households took in boarders, but 40 per cent of these refused to take in women. Landladies complained that girls did not pay as well as men. They spent more of their time in their rooms and therefore wore out the furnishings quicker. They used the bath for a laundry tub and hung up their lingerie in the windows to dry. They were always expecting the use of the electric iron in the kitchen and they kept food in their rooms, which attracted mice. Finally, girls "staying out late or standing in front of the house at night [gave] a bad name to the house."[6]

A new type of assertive woman was emerging in Hamilton, and more conservative people found that difficult to accept. Birth control

Edith, Leona, and Jean catch a bus at Walnut St. in 1923. Buses began to replace the radial lines in the 1920s.

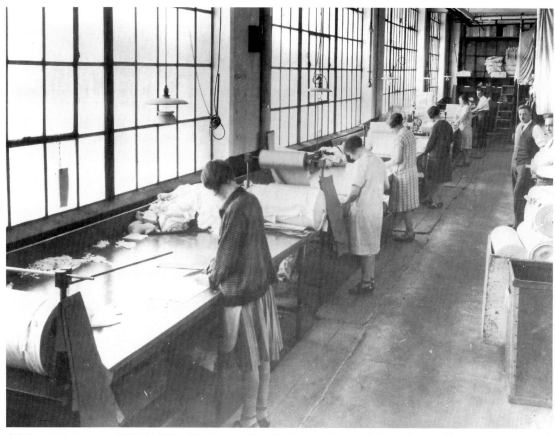

Workers in the Mercury Mills in 1928. Textiles were Hamilton's second-largest industry through this period and employed thousands of women.

information on birth control in Canada, but these women were determined to help the less fortunate. Hawkins and Bagshaw were condemned by the Roman Catholic Bishop as "harlots." He considered their practice "degrading, blasphemous, depraved and atheistic." Others called them "devils" and "whores."[7] But these women had strong support from other women's groups in the city and they never lost their sense of purpose. The police, caught between these two groups, did nothing, which in itself was a strong statement of support.

Another woman in Hamilton in the 1920s who was even more controversial than this was Bessie Starkman, or Bessie Perri as she was usually called. Bessie's story has many different elements to it, but one of the most fascinating is the fact that this woman was an undisputed leader of one of the most notorious criminal gangs in the country. It has long been speculated that one of the reasons that she was murdered was that men in the gang found it difficult to take orders from a woman.

was condemned by virtually all of the churches and politicians of the day, and yet the rapidly declining birth rate suggests that it was practiced by many families. Concern about the effects of poverty on women and children was increasing, and in December 1931 a group of women led by Mrs. Mary Hawkins met to establish Canada's first birth control clinic. In 1932, Dr. Elizabeth Bagshaw became the clinic's medical doctor. At that time, it was illegal to even disseminate

Prohibition and the Perri Gang

For many Protestant leaders at this time the origin of all social problems was "demon rum." They blamed drink for everything from poverty, crime, and debt, to the abandonment of wives and child abuse, and advocated that it was the duty of government to protect its citizens and shield them from harm by prohibiting alcohol. As part of the war effort, the Ontario government passed the Ontario Temperance Act in

Matt Hayes, a local gambler known as "Canada's Diamond Jim Brady," owned the International Hotel on the corner of Barton and James. He was well known for supporting poor North End families in the 1930s.

North, workers could drink, play cards, and shoot craps. High-speed cruisers loaded with whiskey set out from North End boathouses for American ports in the dead of night. One bootlegger even stored liquor and gasoline in caves he dug in the hill that goes down to the harbour from Bay Street.

The most notorious Hamilton bootlegger was Rocco Perri, an Italian immigrant who came to Canada in 1903. He worked in a series of manual jobs and in 1912 was boarding in Toronto with a Jewish family by the name of Starkman. Bessie Starkman left her husband and two children to live with Rocco in St. Catharines. At the time that prohibition began, the couple owned a grocery store on Hess Street North in Hamilton. Soon they were selling whiskey for 50 cents a shot.

By the 1920s, the Perri Gang ran the biggest bootlegging operation in Hamilton, Guelph, Brantford, and the Niagara Peninsula. Some think the gang's operation was the biggest in Canada. Scores of men worked for them. They owned a fleet of speedboats that operated out of Hamilton Harbour and up to 40 souped-up trucks that delivered liquor to outlets in their territory and as far away as Windsor. Once the United States

1916, which introduced prohibition. For many this was the final victory over the evils of drink.

Political support for prohibition came from rural areas, small towns, and the middle class in cities. Hamilton, with its large working class and non-Anglo-Saxon population, was a centre of opposition to the legislation. Soon, there was a thriving illegal trade in liquor and beer, much of it centred in the North End of the city. A number of "blind pigs" (illegal drinking houses) were established close to the factories in the East End. At the "House of Nonsense," on Ferguson Avenue

Prior to the enactment of prohibition in 1917, saloons were the preserve of men.

went dry in 1920 they exported Canadian bonded whiskey across the Niagara Frontier and the Detroit River to their American customers.

In 1920, Rocco and Bessie bought a huge house at 166 Bay Street South with a $2,000 grand piano and a billiard room, where they entertained the city's socialites. Rocco dressed in $200 suits, spats, and silk ties, while Bessie loved expensive jewellery, but they never forgot their origins. Rocco was a big tipper, and the couple often gave money to people in the North End who had fallen on hard times.

Rocco and Bessie developed a rough division of labour in the running of the gang. Rocco supervised the operations side. He was never very far away when a big delivery was being made,

Rocco Perri mourning the death of his wife, Bessie.

he paid the fines when his men were convicted for a violation of the Ontario Temperance Act, and he sometimes tried to pay off the police. Bessie ran the business side of the operation. She placed the orders with the distilleries, including Gooderham and Worts,

Seagram's, and others, and did the banking. The profit on this trade was phenomenal. Through much of prohibition, the couple handled up to 1,000 cases of 60-proof whiskey a day, bought for $18 a case and sold for $80.

Strong religious convictions and practices during this period led to the enactment of prohibition. As a social experiment, however, prohibition was a failure.

In 1924, two murders in Hamilton prompted Rocco to give an interview with *The Toronto Daily Star* to defend himself from the rumours that he had ordered the killings.

While I admit that I am the king of the bootleggers I can assure you that I *have nothing to do with these deaths…. I only give my men fast cars and I sell only the best liquor, so I don't see why anyone should complain, for no one wants prohibition…. Some days I handle 1,000 cases for my customers and the very best families are my customers.*

—*The Toronto Daily Star*, November 19, 1924

Some were outraged by Rocco Perri's statements.

A.H. Lyle, Secretary of the Hamilton Temperance Federation, stated today that the statements made by Rocco Perri in a Toronto paper last night are a challenge to those in charge of the enforcement of the Ontario Temperance Act and should arouse all citizens who favour the enforcement of the law. Continuing, he said, "If I were in a position of authority I would feel it my duty to go the limit to secure a conviction and to put any man who would make such an admission … in jail."

—*The Spectator*, November 20, 1924

Rocco did ultimately spend time in jail for charges linked to this interview. In 1926, a government inquiry into the liquor trade found that Bessie had bank accounts in Hamilton totalling $945,000 — well over $10 million in today's value. At the inquiry, Rocco denied ever giving the interview to the *Toronto Star* and was convicted of perjury. He served six months for the conviction.

Bessie's life came to a premature end on August 13, 1930. The couple had been visiting Rocco's relatives and returned home late at night in their coupe. As Bessie got out to turn on the light in the darkened garage,

…the terrifying deafening report of the first gun was heard. Perri screamed and lunged towards his wife. But the second gun was fired and by that time there was so much smoke in the garage that he could not see whether or not she had fallen. In terror he rushed for the garage door and was in the doorway when the third shot was fired.

—*The Spectator*, August 31, 1946

Bessie's funeral was an unprecedented spectacle. The service, held in the Perri home, was

…interrupted several times by the noise of the huge crowd of people milling about the street in front of the house. The disturbance caused by the shouting throng and the noise of the motor cars striving to force a passage through the crowd, caused the undertaker to come out and call for order from the verandah on two occasions…. At the cemetery, the milling about and the shoving were so great that it was feared some would be pushed into the grave as hundreds sought to catch a glimpse of the expensive ($3,000 silver-trimmed) casket and the sorrowing king of the bootleggers.

—*The Spectator*, August 31, 1946

No one really knows why Bessie was murdered, though James Dubro, an expert on Canadian organized crime, believes it was a result of a narcotics deal that went bad.[8] Rocco fell on hard times after her death, which suggests that she played a crucial role in the gang. It was only after he teamed up with another woman that he was able to regain some of his stature in the criminal underworld. During the war he was interned as an enemy alien and in 1944 he "disappeared." Most people believe that he ended up at the bottom of Hamilton Bay.

Young swimmers from the North End.

That Sporting Life

In August 1930, the very same month that Bessie Perri was murdered and her sensational funeral was held, Hamilton was host to the British Empire Games. Athletes from around the globe came to the city for friendly competition in the new Civic Stadium and the Memorial Swimming Pool in Scott Park. This was the first major sporting event ever held in Canada and it brought international attention to the city.

Hamilton was able to host this event because the city was recognized as a major track and field centre. Captain John Cornelius helped found the Hamilton Olympic Club and trained many of the best athletes of the day. The city hosted the track-team trials for the

Hamiltonians felt great pride when they hosted the British Empire Games in August, 1930. LEFT: A sprint during the games, held in the Civic Stadium (Ivor Wynn Stadium).

1928 and 1932 Olympics. Bobby Robinson, who had managed Canada's track team at the Amsterdam 1928 Olympics, was the person who conceived of the Empire Games and convinced City Council to support them, but the athletes were drawn to the competition by the city's reputation as a major sporting centre.

The 1920s and 1930s saw the movement away from amateur sports to the professional sports that are common today. In the early 1920s Hamilton had its own professional hockey team called the Tigers. Every one of their games would attract 5,000 to 6,000 spectators to the Forum Arena just off Barton Street. In the 1923–24 season it looked like the Tigers were going to win the Stanley Cup, but the players were annoyed because they were paid less than those in other towns. Some games they were not paid at all. Perhaps it was because Hamilton was known as a union town that the Tigers players decided to strike. To beat the strike, the team was taken to New York City by its owners, where it became the basis of the New York Rangers team, of the National Hockey League. Hamilton has not had a big league hockey team since that time.

Football was increasingly becoming the sport with which Hamiltonians identified. After the terrible losses of the First World War it took some time to rebuild the teams in the city, but by 1928 and 1929 the Tigers Football Club again won the Grey Cup and they repeated the win in 1932. By the 1930s, the city had four high schools: Central, Cathedral, Delta, and Westdale, and each of them fielded junior and senior teams. The high school league played

The Grand Opera House was used for theatre, and for sporting events like boxing.

Jack Dempsey, the most famous fighter of his day. Every Friday night there would be a fight card at the Grand Opera House, where the local boys were featured. Perhaps the best was Bobby "Bad News" Eber, a bantamweight. He fought the leading contenders in his weight class, losing only a couple of fights. Eber became the Canadian champion, but he never got a shot at the title. When he went out of town to fight, his fans would follow him. In the midst of the bout, the Tigers' call, "Oskee-Wee-Wee! Oskee-Wa-Wa!" would echo through the hall from far back in the bleachers and the fighter would know that his town was there, cheering for him.

An even more successful boxer who came out of the North End was Jackie Callura. He was one of

Angelo Callura, one of the six boxing Callura brothers.

exciting football, closely followed by many in the city. Hundreds of fans would show up to games and the playoffs attracted thousands. The intense high school rivalry matched the excitement of the competition of the old baseball teams of the late nineteenth century.

The other popular sport of the day was boxing. Boys out of the North End trained with fierce dedication, and some of the best in the sport fought their way to become Canadian champions and challenge the best in the United States. In 1924 Hamilton was so fight-crazy that it merited an exhibition match by none other than

six boxing brothers from an Italian family. Jackie was a tough, aggressive fighter with the image of a poor boy fighting to feed his family. He was a small man, 5'6" and 126 pounds, who fought in the featherweight division, but he was known as the "Belting Bull from Hamilton." By 1931 he had won the Canadian featherweight title, and in

Jack Elliot opened his radio station in 1920. He also owned an airstrip in the East End of the city where he ran a commercial airline and flying school. INSET: Ambrose Summers, a popular radio announcer.

1932 represented Canada in the Los Angeles Olympics. He turned professional in 1936, and in 1943 defeated Jackie Wilson to win the National Boxing Association's world title for his weight class, becoming the first Hamilton boxer to be a world champion. A few months later, he lost the title to Phil Terranora of New York City.

As sport became more professional, theatre and entertainment were also transformed. Hamilton was the scene of some of the most famous vaudeville acts, and on the stage staid Victorian values were replaced by a risqué sauciness. The Marx Brothers, Caruso, and Al Jolson all played here to sell out audiences in the 1920s. From 1918 to the depression, Hamilton was home to 14 theatres: one legitimate theatre, one stock theatre, two vaudeville playhouses, and ten moving picture houses. On October 3, 1921, the Pantages vaudeville theatre opened on King Street East with 3,500 seats. The *Hamilton Herald* described it as a "wonderland, a fairy land of architectural beauty." On opening night, the theatre was filled. It was "a brilliant affair, theatrically, socially, scenically, in every way it was a glorious triumph." (The Pantages was renamed the Palace in 1930, and in 1972 it was demolished.)

The 1920s and '30s brought the mass media to Hamilton, which had a huge impact on local culture. CKOC got its license in 1922. At first it only broadcast with five watts of power, but by 1925 it increased its power and became a commercial station with advertisements. CHML was started by a number of prominent prohibitionists in 1927. About 40 per cent of Hamilton homes had radios by 1932, and listening to "favourite programs," was a common occupation. In the late 1920s, the local movie theatres became controlled by Famous Players and became distribution outlets for Hollywood movies. Not only did this mass media drain away the audience from live theatre, but it also marks a dramatic increase in the Americanization of culture that was happening across Canada.

Cars and Suburbs

The 1920s was the beginning of the automobile age, which had an enormous impact on all North American cities. A modest highway had opened from Hamilton to Toronto by 1917, and by the mid-1920s the city streets were thronged with motor vehicles. The number of cars in Hamilton tripled between 1920 and 1930, and from 1926 to 1930 an average of 30 fatalities and 500 accidents a year occurred in the city.[9] But the motor vehicles brought new mobility. The radial system of electric trams could not withstand the competition from buses, and the lines folded in 1930. Soon, people in cars were commuting longer and longer distances.

A real estate brochure advertising homes in Hamilton.

campaign, the small Baptist college relocated from Toronto to 230 acres in Westdale, on the very edge of Coote's Paradise. At first the growth of the university would be slow, but after the

Westdale became Hamilton's first planned neighbourhood. The community was first proposed in 1912, but it was not until the McKettrick Bridge was built in the 1920s that it was realized. After 1923, active building took place on the curved crescents that bordered on Coote's Paradise, and altogether more than 1,700 homes were built in the neighbourhood. The last lot was sold in the 1940s. Westdale was designed to be an exclusive, middle class community, and when the properties were first sold, covenants restricted the buying of property to people of Anglo Saxon descent.[10] The inherent racism of this was a characteristic of the time, but none the less disturbing.

One development that led to great changes in the city was the building of McMaster University. In 1930, after a six-year

Cars were changing the nature of Hamilton. They could even overcome the barrier of the escarpment with ease.

Westdale Village in the 1930s. Although the cars have changed, the character of the village remains much as it was when it was first built.

Second World War it developed into one of the most important institutions in the city.

Like other progressive cities, Hamilton was influenced by the City Beautiful movement, which advocated planning and parks. In 1917, the city had acquired the 64 acres of land in the east end for Gage Park. The park was later enlarged when the city took over the Gage family home and property known as "The Retreat," and added it to the park. The Retreat is now the Children's Museum. Gage Park

A colourized postcard of the Administration Building at McMaster University, which was opened in 1930.

Hand-tinted glass slides of Gage Park in the 1920s.

remains one of the most beautiful urban parks in the country, with lovely flowerbeds, rolling lawns, and mature trees.

The other spectacular city park acquisition in the 1920s was Coote's Paradise. Tom McQuesten, a City Alderman from an old Hamilton family that owned the gracious Jackson Street mansion, Whitehearn, led the campaign for this park. Coote's Paradise became Hamilton's largest park and the foundation of the Royal Botanical Gardens. It had a total of 377 acres, including 133 acres of water lots, 130 acres of hillside, and 114 acres of level ground. Some of this park has been converted to playing fields, but most of it remains a nature reserve with a proliferation of birds, turtles, deer, and many other species native to the area. McQuesten went on to become the Minister of Highways in the Hepburn government of Ontario in the 1930s. He promoted the Queen Elizabeth Highway, the park system in Niagara Falls, and many other bridges and highways in the province.

As the population expanded through the 1920s, new apartment blocks were built along the main thoroughfares. The art deco Pigott Building, the city's first skyscraper and one of the finest additions to Hamilton's architectural heritage, was opened in March 1929. The

mountain expanded rapidly. By 1929, 6,500 people were living on the brow, but problems arose: Streetlights were so scarce that people went out at night carrying lanterns, and many of the homes were serviced by well water. Typhoid broke out in 1929, and mountain dwellers had to boil their water, but the people loved their neighbourhood.

(Mountain people enjoy the) invigorating climate of the winter months and the cool, balmy breezes of the summer when they loll in the cool shade while their unfortunate brethren are boiling in the sweating city.

—*The Herald*, March 1, 1924

Hard Times

The city prospered in the years from 1923 to 1929, but when the depression struck, the suffering was worse than in most other cities in Ontario because of Hamilton's dependence on heavy industry.[11] "The population shrank from 1931 to 1936, for the first time since the financial crisis of the 1860s. Plant closings also occurred. Companies like National Steel Car, Otis Elevator, and International Harvester had only skeleton crews and the steel companies, Stelco and Dofasco, were operating at 40 to 50 per cent capacity. There were layoffs, reduced hours and decreased wages. Construction projects virtually stopped.

Women tended to do better than men in terms of employment during the depression. The industries that employed a high percentage of women, like clothing, textiles, and food processing, operated at near-capacity levels, but the wages of the women were only about half those of men. There were many families in Hamilton that survived on the wages of their women while the men languished at home hoping to be called back to work.

Welfare legislation was changed in 1930 so that the municipality was only responsible for one-third of the benefits plus the administrative costs. Even with this change, the city struggled to meet its financial obligations. In 1933, in the depths of the depression, almost 25 per cent of Hamilton families were on relief. The system of welfare was restrictive and punitive. Single men were not eligible and many Hamilton boys left home to "ride the rods" of the railways

A block cut showing poverty in Hamilton during the 1930s, by Leonard Hutchinson.

across Canada looking for work. At one time, the city employed 31 welfare investigators. Applicants were closely examined to ensure that they were eligible, and recipients were inspected to ensure they did not drink alcohol or waste money. Those who broke the rules were cut off without any support. Men who were physically fit were required to work for the city a number of days each month. The Rock Gardens at the Botanical Gardens, the Sherman Cut, and other projects were completed using welfare labour.

The high rate of unemployment and the harassment of those on relief led to a sense of hopelessness for many, which turned to bitterness and anger. Political agitation was on the rise. The long lines that stretched from the welfare offices at Victoria Avenue North were places where radicals talked about things like the "injustice of the economic system." Woodward Park in summer was used for political rallies and "education circles." There were marches of the unemployed and demands for better welfare, but little changed before 1940.

The Ontario Workers' Arts and Heritage recently collected accounts from Hamilton people who survived those days. These are some of their stories:

Everyone was so poor. My mother didn't have anything. When we used to go picking fruit we would take mustard sandwiches. That's all she could put on the bloody bread.

—Fred Puser

We had five girls so three slept in one bed and two in another. My two brothers slept together. The pipes from the stove went through the bedrooms so the only heat was from the chimney pipes. You just covered yourself well…. In the Old Guelph Road we didn't have enough blankets or sheets so we put newspapers over us. We were poor people. Oh dear, dear. We were poor.

—Lil Seager

We would go to the market with our baskets on Saturday when it was closing time and say, 'Have you got anything you don't want?' We would get potatoes, a cabbage…. Like, you have no idea how long you could eat off those. Everybody preserved…. You never bought strawberry jam. It was always homemade. We always had a small vegetable garden for our tomatoes, cucumbers. Not anything was ever, ever wasted.

—Florence Fisher

Hutchinson, a Hamilton artist, captured the despair of the unemployed during the Great Depression.

sell it.' My dad used to work two days a week for welfare, cleaning parks and building the Sherman Avenue Cut.

I recall standing in line at the welfare office with my mother down on Victoria Avenue and going in there and having Capelli, his name was, everyone hated him but he was just doing his job, examine your shoes. And they'd give you a new pair of boots. To this day I can't wear boots cause those welfare boots ruined my feet.

—Floyd Read

In the summertime we used to hold meetings in Woodlands Park in the noon hour. A big gang used to come out and eat in the park…. We used to have the sound truck there and tell them about the union.

—Bert McClure

(My dad) would get up every morning and head out to look for work and when it got noon time my mom would say to me. 'Go to the park and wake your dad up and tell him to come home for lunch.' There was no work.

When we were on welfare they used to come and check out your coal bin. They would come through your house and say, 'You don't need that chair. Go

My dad told me this story. He was at a meeting in Woodlands Park with Tim Buck and the Communists and all of a sudden a bunch of firemen came in and they had nozzles on their hoses and they wailed into this crowd and drove them out of the park with the water hoses because that's the way they handled things in those days. He hated firemen after that.

—Fred Puser

The following letter speaks with a quiet eloquence of the despair of one Hamilton woman. It was written by Miss Elizabeth McCrae to Prime Minister R.B. Bennett and dated April 6, 1934.

Dear Prime Minister:

I am writing you as a last resource to see if I cannot, through your aid, obtain a position and at last, after a period of more than two years, support myself and enjoy again a little independence.

The fact is this day I am faced with starvation and I see no possible means of counteracting or even averting it temporarily!

If you require references of character or ability I would suggest that you write to T. M. Sanderson of Essex, Ontario. I worked as stenographer and bookkeeper with him for over three years in the office of the Sanderson-Marwick Co., Ltd., in Essex. I feel certain that you have made his acquaintance for he was President of the Conservative Association at the time of the banquet held in your worshipful honour a few years ago.

I have received a high school and business-college education and I have had experience as a librarian. My business career has been limited to insurance, hosiery, and public stenography, each time in the capacity of bookkeeper and stenographer.

My father is a farmer at Pilot Mound, Manitoba and during the past years his income has been nil, so I cannot get any assistance from him. In fact, until I joined the list of unemployed I had been lending the folks at home my aid. To save my mother from worry I have continually assured her that I am working and till the end I will save her from distress by sticking to this story.

When the Sanderson-Marwick Co. Ltd., went out of business I had saved a little money and, there being no work there for me, I came to Hamilton. Since then I have applied for every position that I heard about but there were always so many girls who applied that it was impossible to get work. So time went on and my clothing became very shabby. I was afraid to spend the little I had to replenish my wardrobe. Always the fear was before me that I would fail to get the position and then I would be without food and a roof over my head in a short time. Many prospective employers just glanced at my attire and shook their heads and more times than I care to mention I was turned away without a trial. I began to cut down on my food and I obtained a poor but respectable room at $1 per week.

First I ate three very light meals a day; then two and then one. During the past two weeks I have eaten only toast and drunk a cup of tea every other day. In the past fortnight I have lost 20 pounds and the result of this deprivation is that I am so very nervous that I could never stand a test along with one, two and three hundred girls. Today I went to an office for an examination and the examiner just looked me over and said; "I am afraid, Miss, you are so awfully shabby I could never have you in my office."

I was so worried and disappointed and frightened that I replied somewhat angrily: "Do you think clothes can be picked up in the streets?"

"Well," he replied with aggravating insolence, "lots of girls find them there these days."

Mister Bennett, that almost broke my heart. Above everything else I have been very particular about my friends and since moving here I have never gone out in the evening and the loneliness is hard to bear, but oh, sir, the thought of starvation is driving me mad!

Day after day I pass the delicatessen and the food in the window looks oh so good! So tempting and I'm so hungry. Yes I am very hungry and the stamp which carries this letter to you will represent the last three cents I have in the world, yet before I will stoop to dishonour my family, my character or my God I will drown myself in the Lake.

Oh please sir, can you do something for me? Can you get me a job anywhere in the Dominion of Canada? I wouldn't mind if I could just lie down and die but to starve, oh its terrible to think about.

Mr. Bennett, even if you can do nothing for me I want to thank you for your kindness in reading this letter and if I were jobless and semi-hungry for a life time I would still be a Conservative to the last and fight for that Government.

Thanking you again for your very kind attention. I am, your humble servant,

Miss Elizabeth McCrae[12]

The depression haunted the memories of those that lived through it. Not only did the ten lost years of the '30s shape the events of the war and the decades that came after it, but it left the survivors with the determination that never again should people be forced to experience the hardship and insecurity of those years.

Chapter Seven

FROM WAR TO GOOD TIMES
(1940 – 1960)

The Great Depression and the Second World War did more to shape our world than any other set of events. They laid the foundations for the Cold War that lasted for 45 years and forged social and economic policies that brought levels of stability and prosperity that were unprecedented. But these international events also changed the outlook of ordinary people in Hamilton.

I'd been through hell on the battlefields of France, Belgium and Holland and I was damned if I was going to take it from a bunch of foremen at Stelco.

Being in the Navy changed my attitude. We were fighting for freedom and a better kind of living, freedom of speech and rights. When I came back I would say, "Nobody's going to push me around."

They came back with a lot of different ideas than they went away with. A serviceman in 1945 was looked up to.
—Quotes from three Hamilton Steelworkers[1]

VJ Night, 1945 *by Frank Panabaker.*

The War

When war broke out on September 1, 1939, it was not met with the excitement of August 1914. People in Hamilton knew what war was like and greeted it with trepidation, and yet within a short period of time the two local regiments had recruited enough men to bring them up to strength. The Royal Hamilton Light Infantry (RHLI), or the "Rileys," as they were affectionately known, had soon signed up 1,500 men. The Argyll and Sutherland Highlanders set up a recruiting tent in Gore Park, the centre of recruiting efforts during the First World War, and reached their full complement of men in 16 days.

In this war, men did not rush to get overseas. The RHLI trained in Canada and went overseas in 1941. They continued their training in southern England. Finally, on August 19, 1942, 550 men of the regiment set off on what most thought was another routine exercise. They boarded ships at Southampton along with a number of other Canadian units and set off towards France and the town of Dieppe.

The Dieppe Raid remains one of the most controversial events of the Second World War. Everything went wrong. The Rileys were to take part in the frontal assault of the beach and the main esplanade of the town. The men, with all of their equipment, were dropped off into three feet of water and had to wade ashore. The Germans were up on the cliffs and raked the beach with murderous machine gun fire. Other Canadian flanking units that were to knock out these guns were pinned down on the

Hamilton soldiers saw some of the heaviest fighting during the Second World War.

A recruiting poster.

beach. The Calgary Tanks, who were to lead the assault into the town, could not get traction in the loose pebbles of the beach and became sitting ducks for the big German guns. A group of the RHLI made it up over a ten-foot high concrete seawall, through the barbed wire on top of the wall, and to their objective of the Casino, but then the Germans counterattacked.

The retreat was even more disastrous. Radios were knocked out so that the withdrawal was uncoordinated. Men gathered on the beach, huddling behind burned out vehicles for protection from the withering fire, as they waited for the landing craft to pick them up. Hundreds drowned in the rising tide. Of the 550 officers and men of the RHLI who went into the battle, 201 died, 257 were taken prisoner and spent the next two years and nine months in a German prison of war camp, and 92 made it back to England, including many who were seriously wounded. More than 900 Canadians lost their lives on the beaches and 1,400 were taken prisoner, making Dieppe the most tragic day for Canada in the entire Second World War.

It is believed that the model for this poster was a Hamilton man.

The Argyll and Sutherland Highlanders went to Niagara-on-the-Lake for training and then spent almost a year of garrison duty in Jamaica. They finally went overseas to Europe in July 1943. The Argylls went ashore in Normandy on July 21, 1944 and were in the front lines until the end of the war as they fought through France, Belgium, Holland, and into Germany. They were involved in a series of important battles: Falaise, Caen, Möderbrugg, and Hochwald. At the end of the war men from the pipes and drums of the regiment provided the music as the British flag was raised over Berlin. The regiment suffered over 800 casualties in the war.

After Dieppe, the RHLI was brought back to full complement with replacements. On July 5, 1944 they landed in France, four weeks after D-day, and fought in the front lines through to Holland. They were involved in the attack at Verrières in France, the heavy fighting around Woensdrecht, and gruelling battles of the Rhineland.

Hamilton contributed more than two regiments to the war effort. Men joined the navy and served in the Battle of the North Atlantic and a large number were in the Air Force, either as aircrew or on the ground. Women played an important role in all three branches of the armed services. Hamilton even became a training centre for the air force during the war. Sixteen hundred acres of land were expropriated in Mount Hope in 1940 for an airport. Runways were laid down and two large temporary hangars were built. For the next three years, the Mount Hope airport trained in excess of 15,000 air force personnel from all over the British Empire. The skies were filled with droning aircraft, and airmen were familiar figures on the streets of Hamilton.

The Home Front

As the momentum of the war began to pick up, Hamilton industry was transformed. Factories which had been working at between 20 and 40 per cent capacity during the depression, were suddenly called on to work at full production. By 1942, 60,000 workers were labouring in Hamilton industries, 20,000 in munitions production alone, and most were working far more than a 40-hour week. A

Women industrial workers during the Second World War.

serious labour shortage had developed by 1941. Like in the First World War, women were recruited to work in the heavy industries, and many workers from the Maritimes, Quebec, and the Prairie Provinces came to Hamilton to take up employment in the booming plants. A survey found that, by 1942, there was a serious housing shortage in the city.[2]

During the First World War, government inactivity led to inflation and economic hardship. This time, the government tried to control the Canadian economy. There were controls on wages, and later a system of rationing was introduced. Gasoline was difficult to get, and only people in essential jobs were allowed to buy tires or cars.

As part of the government's system of economic controls, it created a crown corporation to try to meet the housing crisis that had developed in cities. The corporation was called Wartime Housing Limited and Joseph Pigott, the head of the Hamilton firm Pigott Construction, was appointed to run it. In Hamilton, dormitory halls for single men were built, which had recreational facilities. Over 1,700

Artist Frank Panabaker's vision of the steel complex after the war.

After the Second World War, affordable housing construction led to an increase in home ownership.

temporary wartime housing units were built for families in the east end and on the mountain, but overcrowding remained a serious problem.

When the war was over and the boys came home, there was an intense outpouring of joy because every Canadian felt they had made a contribution to winning this terrible conflict. It is estimated that 20,000 Hamiltonians served in the armed forces and of that number 4,000 were killed, were missing in action, or returned home wounded. When the Royal Hamilton Light Infantry arrived home on November 22, 1945 the city went wild.

Deafening cheers went up about the station as the train pulled in. Battalion personnel who got back earlier waved and shouted from the station plaza; the colour party was drawn to attention; ticker tape fluttered from the station into the street, and bands played the stirring regimental march, "Mountain Rose." (Then) battalion personnel heard the familiar strains of "Johnny Comes Marching Home" over the long shrill whistling of the locomotive and waved from the windows to cheering crowds below.

—*The Spectator*, November 22, 1945

The Argylls came home to an equally rousing reception.

VE Day Parade. When victory was declared in Europe in 1945, the people of Hamilton took to the streets in celebration.

The troops took up parade formation on the ramp before starting the last lap of their long journey, marching between cheering rows of citizens and beneath showers of ticker tape and confetti swirling at King and James....
It was in the crowded decorated armouries that the veterans received their most tumultuous welcome. As the head of the column entered, cheering was sustained while the regiment took up positions.... Seconds after the colours had been marched off and the National Anthem sung, the armouries was a bedlam as the men broke ranks and rushed to meet loved ones. There was a lot of laughter, some tears, a little bewilderment on the part of the very young, some of whom may have never seen or only vaguely remembered the big men in uniform who took them in their arms.

—The Spectator, January 19, 1946

The men of the city made one other remarkable contribution to the war. The Crerars were an old Hamilton family, prominent in business, politics and social welfare. Henry Crerar was born and raised in the city. He attended Royal Military College and was an artillery officer in the First World War. In the Second World War, he became a full general and led the Canadian troops and other units in their campaign through northern France, Belgium and Holland. J.L. Granatstein called him: "unquestionably the most important Canadian soldier of the Second World War." On October 10, 1946 General Crerar returned home and was given a thunderous welcome by 20,000 people in Civic Stadium.

The experience of the two world wars was quite different for Hamiltonians. In the first war, the men were sent off with rousing cheers and returned home to silence. In the Second World War, they had left Hamilton with anxiety and trepidation and returned to cheers. The two wars changed attitudes. People in the services had travelled and were more international in their outlook. In Hamilton the memories of the depression, when conditions had stagnated for "Ten Lost Years," were still vivid in people's minds and they were determined to make a better world.

The 1946 Strike

During the depression and war, the wages and conditions of work in the large factories of Hamilton continued to be difficult. These are the recollections of steelworkers who worked for the Steel Company of Canada:

February 1935 I started in the 10–12 mill (at Stelco) — steady nights. I didn't mind that part of it but you'd pack your lunch and go down and they'd say, "You stay, you stay, you stay," and the rest would go home. I think my first pay I got $12 for two weeks. That meant I was workin' about three days a week. I got sick

The open-air market adjacent to City Hall continued to be a major downtown attraction, as shown in Henry Smith's 1958 painting, Hamilton Market.

United Electrical Workers organizing their picket lines during the 1946 Westinghouse strike.

my job at the office of the superintendent and I went in and I said I was quittin' and he said what for, and I said there was a lot of bull goin' on around here. So I told him and showed him where the baskets were of booze and stuff. He got mad about it and after that things were better in the department.

—Reg Gisborn

A new supervisor came in and removed every ethnic worker from key jobs and replaced them with Anglo-Saxons.... I replaced a person I thought to be a truly great man, a big Pole, twice as big as I am, strong and hard working, and absolutely fearful of any form of supervision. The company couldn't have had a better man. He was the kindest person to me, a seventeen-year old kid, trying to hold up my end on a ten-and-half hour night shift. This man did everything to help me, and it was just terrible the way I had to take his job. I didn't want to do it and in fact I went into the office, with my cap off by the way, and told the superintendent that it was unfair. He told me to get out on the job or get the hell out of the plant. The supervisors had absolute authority and they used it ruthlessly.

—John Lisson

of it cause I could see how the others got on. I found that some of them would bring the foremen bottles of wine and groceries and they would set them down behind a machine for him. So after about a month and a half I was to line up for

Sam Lawrence was an ardent trade unionist. This picture shows him picketing during the 1930s. He was a longtime member of Hamilton city council and mayor during the 1946 strikes.

The ethnic types (on the slag dump) were actually in mortal fear. I'd be working right alongside of them and I could see them start to shake and you'd turn around and there would be the foreman…. The foreman was God down there.

—Jake Isbister

Unions had been active at the Steel Company since 1919, but they were craft unions that only organized skilled workers. The idea of industrial-style unions that would organize all the workers in a plant regardless of skill was advocated by some, but many felt that this was a radical or communist idea. In 1936, the sheet mill workers staged a two-week strike that resulted in better pay for the workers in that mill. At that same time a group of unionists in the United States, led by the president of the United Mine Workers, John L. Lewis, set up a group called the Committee for Industrial Organization (CIO), and the unionists in the sheet mill dedicated themselves to organizing all the workers in the plant. They became members of the Steel Workers Organizing Committee (SWOC), which later became the United Steelworkers of America.

The struggle to organize the workers at the Steel Company of Canada through the depression and the war was of almost epic proportions. It involved hundreds of workers who collected union dues while they avoided the ever-present foremen. Secret meetings were held in houses and restaurants, and leaflets handed out at the plant gates during shift changes. These were risky activities. Unionists who were discovered sometimes lost their jobs and others were demoted, but still they doggedly kept up the work and kept up the pressure on the company.

Once the war began and an acute labour shortage developed in Hamilton, the unionists began to feel more confident and aggressive, but intense conflict continued. After the Italian government became the ally of the Germans in the war, the RCMP came into Stelco and insisted that about 200 Italians be fired and others removed from sensitive jobs because they were considered a security risk. This led to even greater resentment by ethnic workers in the plant. The federal government wanted to control every aspect of the economy for the war effort, and it had a great fear of strikes and work disruptions. On

A working-class neighbourhood at York and McGill Streets, as it looks today.

and business circles that the depressed economic conditions that followed the First World War would develop again. This led to a determination to hold the line against wage increases. The workers and the unions that represented them, on the other hand, were determined to gain union security and to make the economic gains that had eluded them for so long.

Both sides prepared for a struggle in the spring and early summer of 1946. Local 1005 put forward four basic demands: an increase in wages of 19 1/2 cents an hour (from $30.96 to $33.60 a week base pay), a 40-hour week, two weeks paid vacation after five years, and union security with automatic deduction of union dues (the so-called union shop). The company countered by saying the union demands broke the government controls and guidelines. They offered a 5 1/2 cent an hour wage increase, but were vehemently opposed to union check off. Finally, the union announced that if the company did not agree to its members' demands, they would strike on July 15, 1946.

The tensions on both sides were intense. On July 8, the company increased its offer to 10 cents an hour and demanded the government hold a secret vote on the proposal. The union ridiculed the offer. On July 11, four days before the strike deadline, the government suddenly acted by seizing the steel plant and issuing an order-in-council outlawing the strike. Charlie Millard, the Canadian President of the Steelworkers, attacked the decision.

So far as I can gather the government is quite prepared to rush to the side of the employer and throw overboard the whole democratic process of collective bargaining.

—*The Spectator*, July 11, 1946

Workers taking a break during the postwar period.

February 1, 1943 a number of strikes took place across the country, and in response the government enacted legislation in January 1944, which for the first time gave workers the right to organize into unions, and allowed the certification of bargaining units and compulsory collective bargaining. This permitted Local 1005 of the Steelworkers, as the union at Stelco was now called, to be certified as the agent to represent the workers and led to the first contract between the union and the Steel Company in February 1945.

In the months after the end of the war, a confrontation between labour and the large employers in Hamilton grew. Hugh Hilton, the president of Stelco, accused the union of having "communistic associations," while the union denounced the autocratic style of the company. At the conclusion of the war concern arose in government

It then became clear that the company was making its own preparations for a strike by bringing in bunk beds, stockpiling food and building an airfield within the company property. Employees were being asked if they would stay in the plant if a strike occurred. The union was in the difficult position that if they struck they would be defying the law, but if they caved in they would lose their union and many members would lose their jobs.

Finally, on the evening of July 14, the unionists and their supporters met in the Playhouse Cinema on Sherman Avenue North to discuss their situation. In the overheated atmosphere of the crammed theatre, rousing speeches were delivered by one union leader after another. Then, "suddenly the doors opened, the crowd came out of the theatre, and they all marched north on Sherman Avenue to Burlington, and right to the Wilcox Gate. The strike was on!"[3]

The choice to strike or to stay in the plant was a difficult one for many of the workers. In the end, somewhere between 1,000 and 1,500 workers stayed inside the plant. Of that number, some 500 were foremen and superintendents and the rest were workers.

It was the foreign people who were the backbone of the strike: the Poles, Ukrainians, and Italians. They were the ones who came out solid.... The Canadian born weren't bad, but it was the English, Scotch and Irish who stayed in. They had the best jobs and a lot of them hated the union.

—A Steelworker[4]

In the record-breaking heat of the summer of 1946, strikes took place at four large concerns in Hamilton: Stelco, Westinghouse, Firestone, and the *Spectator*, but it was the strike at Stelco that captured the attention of the public. Here was a clear polarization between a militant industrial union and a large, powerful Canadian corporation that wanted to run its plant in the old, authoritarian way. The media of the day was attracted to the confrontation and reported on it daily.

On July 16, Hilton, the president of Stelco, hosted a media tour of the plant showing how steel was continuing to be produced. Claims and counter claims were made as to how many men were in the plant. The unionists tried to persuade the men inside to come out, and daubed some of their houses with paint in big letters reading "SCAB." In the middle of the night of July 16–17, the company tried

The York St. neighbourhood as it looked just after the war.

to run a train loaded with steel through the picket line. As the train approached the line, 300 men attacked the strikers with rocks, pick handles, and rubber hoses. Shouts rang out as other picketers ran to

Italian women served spaghetti to the picketers every Saturday night during the 1946 Stelco strike.

reinforce the line, hurling the rocks back and pushing and shoving the strikebreakers. Four police cars arrived, but the battle raged for half an hour before the train retreated back inside the plant.

The Whisper — *the steelworker's navy during the 1946 Stelco strike.*

The next day, Police Chief Crocker made the telling comment:

If the Steel Company doesn't force our hand, my opinion is that the steel strike will be conducted in an orderly manner.

—*The Spectator*, July 17, 1946

Four days after the strike began, Mayor Sam Lawrence spoke to a union rally in Woodlands Park. He left no doubt as to his feelings about the strike.

I am a labour man first and a chief magistrate second…. I want to raise my voice in protest against the most vicious Order-in-Council that is denying the workers the right to strike."

—*The Spectator*, July 18, 1946

A few days later, both union and management were called to testify before a Parliamentary committee. Hugh Hilton, the company president, was the only spokesman for Stelco. The sheer stubborn toughness of the man stunned the Members of Parliament, journalists, and public alike: "I began work at 17, worked for 17½ cents an hour, 12 hours a day, seven days a week. I just kept on and here I am." He was blunt, confrontational, and disparaging of the union. Describing the situation in Hamilton, he said it "beggars description with lawlessness rampant and people intimidated, with families of loyal honest workers terrorized." He felt that government was "derelict unless it compelled respect for the law and made the men get back to work."[5] This had become the crux of the issue: Would the government use its power to side with the company and break the steel strike with the use of force?

As the strike progressed, an underlying sense of tension and excitement developed. The huge picket line constantly circled the Wilcox Gate. Spectators from across the city came down to watch. Wives brought their children, who would join their fathers walking on the picket line. The Christmas Sisters, married to two bothers on the line, provided entertainment with numbers such as "Scab Song," which they had composed; Pete Seeger entertained the picket line; and exhibitions of professional wrestling were put on by the likes of Whipper Billy Watson. Once a week, a big spaghetti supper was put on by the Italian women. A sense of camaraderie that had never existed in the plant developed on the picket line.

But it was not all easy. Men patrolled the huge perimeter of the Stelco plant, watching for scabs slipping through the lines. There were beatings, though no one was seriously hurt. The company rented a

City Controller Nora Francis Henderson confronting the steelworkers' picket line in the 1946 Stelco strike.

boat to ferry supplies into the plant, so the union got the loan of a launch called the *Whisper* that had been used in the bootlegging trade. "The Union Navy," as the strikers who manned the launch called themselves, often got into trouble as they tried to harass the company boat. There was even an aerial dogfight in the strike. The union rented an aircraft and one of the strikers who had flown 85 missions over Europe went up and dropped leaflets to the men inside the plant. The company had their own airplane and it climbed into the sky and buzzed the union plane. Never before or since has there been a strike fought on land, sea and air.

The issue of lawlessness had not been resolved. Nora Francis Henderson, a Hamilton Controller who had been the first woman elected to council, attacked Mayor Lawrence for siding with the strikers. She deplored the "state of lawlessness" and demanded that the police be brought in to open the picket line. On August 2, she marched alone to the picket line and demanded to be allowed into the plant. The picture of this small woman surrounded by a sea of large

The union plane leafletting the men who continued to work in the plant during the strike.

The veterans' march on August 26, 1946 supporting the steelworkers' strike.

contentious issue. Thousands of strikers and their supporters descended on City Hall on James Street North. The galleries were packed and the streets teeming with people. Whenever Mayor Lawrence and council members who supported the union spoke, their supporters cheered, and whenever Nora Francis Henderson and members of her faction spoke, her supporters cheered and the unionists booed. When the meeting was over and Henderson went outside, the crowd turned ugly and sang: "We'll hang Nora Francis to a sour apple tree." As she got into her car, it looked for a moment as though it would be turned over by the unruly crowd, but union men intervened and she drove away peacefully.

steelworkers became a symbol for all those who believed the police should be brought in to "restore order." The union avoided a confrontation and allowed her to pass, but when she came out she argued even more vehemently. "What burns me up is that 2,700 men inside the plant are denied free access to the municipality."[6]

A few days later, a city council meeting was held to deal with this

The once-solid picket lines were beginning to look frayed and impatient. Men were losing their tempers. Trucks were overturned. Union commandos slipped through the lines into the plant at night and committed acts of sabotage. Finally, on August 23, a resolution was put before City Council to bring in police reinforcements. Mayor

Sam Lawrence spoke against it, but it passed. The provincial government sent 250 OPP officers and the federal government an additional 250 RCMP. Hamilton restaurant workers refused to serve the police if they came in uniform, but it looked as if the government had allied itself with the company and was preparing to break the strike with force.

The tension in the city was palpable when, on August 26, 10,000 veterans gathered to march in support of the union and the strike. The parade was larger than any military gathering that had ever marched through the streets of Hamilton. The men lined up, some in their old army jackets with their decorations and rank proudly showing. Officers out in front of platoons, sergeants and corporals in positions, the men lined up in ranks, row upon row. They marched through the streets, old comrades in arms, ready for the next battle if one was to come; they paraded down to the picket line and the Wilcox Gate. For a moment, it seemed as though they would just keep on marching right into the plant and seize it as if the place rightfully belonged to them, but they stopped, and gradually the march dispersed. The message of the march was very clear. These men had sacrificed for their country. Many just like them had given their lives. And now they were prepared to fight for what they believed in once again. The politician who ordered the police to break the strike would have the blood of these veterans on his hands because violence would be inevitable.

The order for the police to open the picket line never came. Slowly the strike wore on until Charlie Millard, the president of the Steelworkers' Union, was able to reach a settlement with the company. Both sides compromised, but when the men went back into the plant on October 4, 1946, they went back with a sense of victory and accomplishment. They had won union security, the most important of their demands. A different world lay ahead.

The accomplishments of the '46 strike belonged to the unions, but the outcome affected people far beyond the union members. To workers and management alike, the results of the strike came to symbolize that the old autocratic ways would not be tolerated any more. People expected to be treated with dignity and respect, and they expected to be paid a living wage. Even in non-unionized companies, these principles were accepted. Time has shown that this is the enduring victory of the strike.

Evelyn Dick on her way to her first trial.

The Evelyn Dick Murder Trial

At the same time that the '46 strike was going on, Hamilton gained national attention as the location of one of the most notorious murder trials of the century. The dismembered body of John Dick was discovered on March 16 by two children at Mount Albion Falls. A few days later police announced that they had found the partly decomposed body of a baby in the attic of the Dick home. The baby had been strangled with butcher twine. Evelyn Dick, her lover William Bohozuk, and her parents, Mr. and Mrs. Donald MacLean, were all charged with murder.

Evelyn Dick ultimately had three trials, and the evidence was a sensation. Up to 6,000 people would show up on the street to cheer and jeer at the participants. Members of the press from across North America attended the trial. Adding to the allure, Evelyn was a beautiful young woman who would be escorted to the courthouse wearing expensive clothes. Her father, an employee of the Hamilton Street Railway, was shown to have stolen at least $2,500 worth of tram tickets, but the real shock came when it was disclosed that Evelyn had been supported in lavish style by a number of prominent Hamilton men. Rumours sped through the community, and no doubt many feared that their names might become attached to this notorious crime.

In the end, no names were revealed. The charges against

Bohozuk and Mrs. MacLean were dropped because Evelyn refused to testify against them. Evelyn Dick was initially convicted of the murder of her husband, but in her third trial she was defended by a lawyer who went on to become one of the most famous defense attorneys in Canada, J.J. Robinette. The conviction was overturned. She was ultimately convicted of the lesser charge of manslaughter in the death of the child and was sentenced to life imprisonment. Her father, Donald MacLean was convicted as an accessory after the fact and sentenced to five years.

Boom Times

The fears of government and business that a depression would develop after the war never materialized. Just the opposite happened, in fact. Demand had been pent up for a long time, and now that people had some money they spent it on consumer goods, cars, and houses. Industry boomed, and by 1960 incomes had more than doubled, workers had more job security, and work was less seasonal. Young people married and the birth rate soared to the point where the term "baby boomers" has been given to the generation born right after the Second World War.

In Hamilton, it was the steel companies that expanded rapidly. Dofasco's output grew 400 per cent between 1945 and 1960, while Stelco more than doubled its output from 1950 to 1962. Much of the demand for steel was coming from the rapidly expanding auto industry. Hamilton got its own automobile plant in 1948 with the opening of Studebaker. Other industries did not fare as well as steel, however. The

The band at the Brant Inn, a popular and elegant dance hall in Burlington. For people who had suffered through the Depression and Second World War, the prosperity of the late '40s and '50s was more than a welcome relief. It was a time to celebrate.

International Harvester plant never grew beyond 3,000 employees. Other companies expanded, but they opened plants in other centres and their Hamilton operations remained about the same size. The textile industry shrank dramatically as it faced increasing competition. In 1941, 15 per cent of all manufacturing jobs in

Hamilton were in the spinning and knitting mills. Most of the mills had closed by 1960, and textile workers made up only a small part of the workforce.[7]

These boom times attracted new people to the city, who found work in the expanding industries. British immigration was high, and many skilled workers were recruited from the United Kingdom to work in industry. Right after the Second World War, a number of refugees who fled from countries occupied by the Soviet Union settled in Hamilton. These included Poles, Ukrainians, Hungarians, Czechoslovakians, Serbs, Lithuanians, Estonians, and Latvians. Most of these people were strongly anti-communist and they changed the politics of their communities. After 1950, Italians came to Hamilton in great numbers; by 1961, 17,500 were living in the city and a large number of them came from the small Sicilian town of Racalmutto. By 1960 Hamilton had a distinctly multicultural character. Many of the first generation families lived in the North End, along York Street or in the communities along Barton Street in the east end of the city. Ethnic cultural groups multiplied, and community churches often had their own clergy and built buildings to serve their communities. By 1960, Catholics were the largest religious denomination in the city.

The changes in the city of Hamilton brought a new interest in culture. Professional theatre and vaudeville had died in the 1930s, but music found new life. In 1949, the Hamilton Philharmonic Orchestra was formed under the direction of Jan Wolanek. Amateur theatre

Looking South, James Street, Hamilton *by Juanita le Barre Symington.*

grew as the Players' Guild put on six or seven productions a year.

McMaster University expanded rapidly and developed an enviable reputation, particularly in the physical sciences and engineering. The university became a non-denominational institution in 1957, and continued its strong academic tradition in the humanities and social sciences. Not only did it have large and growing undergraduate programs, but increasing numbers of

Radio, and later television, brought entertainment into the homes of Hamilton families. Live theatre virtually disappeared and even some of the big movie cinemas fell on hard times.

graduate students came to McMaster, which helped to spawn a rich cultural life centred around the university. Westdale was beginning to take on the look of a college town, with professors and students as a permanent fixture.

One of the most unusual cultural developments was television. Ken Soble had come to Hamilton in 1936 as the manager of CHML. He bought the station in 1943 and converted it into a truly community radio station. He increased the broadcast power and focused on local news and events. In the 1946 strike, for example, CHML broadcast programs both from inside the plant and on the picket lines. September 1952 marks the first television broadcast in Canada, when CBC Toronto and Montreal went on the air. Soble argued that Hamilton needed its own station and used all of his considerable political influence to ensure that his company was granted a license.

It was a huge undertaking to establish a TV station in a mid-sized city, but Soble accomplished it. A monster-sized 540-foot high broadcast tower was built, a studio was constructed in the old Southam mansion on Jackson Street, and on June 7, 1954, the first show went on the air. The station's shows reflected Soble's style by featuring local talent. That first night, the performers included a Hungarian pianist; the Dofasco male choir; Patti Ellis, "a pert young songstress;" a dancing team of Jackie Kay and Eddie Dunnette, and the Hamilton public school festival choir under Cyril Hampshire. Another high point was the recitation of the winning essay: "What Canada Means to Me." The newspaper account reported that an "air of jubilation swept the station staff" when it went on the air.[8]

Sport was changing as well. The high schools continued with their intense competition, particularly in football, basketball, and track and field. Football was increasingly becoming Hamilton's passion. In the late '40s, most of the players were local Hamilton boys who worked full time in factories and were paid between $50 and $80 a game. By 1960, the sport had become professionalized. The best university players from across Canada were recruited, and top American players were brought in. The Tiger Cats still drew local pride, but no longer was it a team of local boys going out to play the boys from other centres. The Tiger Cats were becoming a part of the growing entertainment industry.

Hamilton was rapidly changed as well. From 1930 to 1945, virtually no building was done in the city, but with the return of boom times people bought cars, workers could get mortgages and purchased houses. Virtually all of the land under the mountain was taken up by low-density housing, so a

CHCH, Hamilton's own television station, began broadcasting on June 7, 1954.

John Holland

In 1954, when the American South was still segregated and dominated by the Klu Klux Klan, Hamilton gave its "Citizen of the Year" award to the Reverend John Holland, the pastor of the Stewart Memorial, an African Methodist Episcopal Church on John Street North.

John Holland's parents had been born slaves in Maryland and escaped to Canada on the Underground Railway. His father Tom had returned to fight in the Union Army during the Civil War and then settled in Hamilton. Tom Holland owned a feed store on Mary Street. The family was very poor but deeply religious. As a young man, John wanted to become a minister, but the family could not afford the cost of his education, so he became a railway porter with the TH&B, one of the few occupations open to Black men early in the century.

Blacks faced prejudice and constant racial slurs. Holland once told a magazine writer: "In those days a coloured boy had either to be a good fighter or a good runner and I was pretty good at both." Ray Lewis, a Hamilton Olympic athlete who was also a Black man raised in Hamilton, said of those days, "We had to be careful. We had to be smart. [John Holland] was both. He was a man who conducted himself well at all times. This was not always easy to do. Sometimes you wanted to knock them on their ass."

John Holland was quickly promoted in his job as a railway porter, but in his spare time he studied to be an ordained minister.

In 1924, at the age of 42 he received ordination and became the assistant minister of the Episcopal Church on John Street North, a church congregation descended from the early Black churches on Concession Street. In 1937, with the death of the pastor Claude Stewart, the name of the church was changed to Stewart Memorial and John Holland became its pastor.

For several years, Holland kept his job with the TH&B, and on Sundays and in every spare moment he preached and tended to the needs of the congregation. The hardships of the Black community during the 1930s were severe. When the Second World War began, Black men were denied the right to join the Canadian Army, but soon many were hired to work in the big plants. In 1948, after 33 years as a porter, John Holland retired and devoted himself full time to the work of his church. Ray Lewis described him in these words: "He really had the people of Hamilton in his heart and he lived by it. There's never been another one like him. I don't know anybody who's done for the coloured people in town what he has."

Five months after he received the medal for Citizen of the Year in 1954, John Holland died. Norman Rawson, who officiated at the funeral, said: "[Stewart Memorial] was filled to the doors. The humble, the poor, the rich and socially elite were all there. Sorrow was written on every face. We had all lost a beloved friend."[9]

rapid expansion occurred on the mountain. In 1953, and again in 1960, large chunks of farmland on the mountain were annexed by the city to accommodate growth. Other land was annexed in the east and west ends. Commuting to and from work by car became the norm for many people. Drivers complained about congestion, and on October 28, 1956, the one-way street system was instituted. The old neighbourhoods under the mountain, which had been built in earlier days, now had streams of cars hurtling along the streets. The downtown, which had always been the vital business and commercial centre of the city, showed signs of serious decay by 1960. The public and the politicians talked about it endlessly. Something had to be done to rescue the retail core of the city.

Chapter Eight

THE DECADES OF CONTROVERSY (1960 – 1980)

*People didn't recognize at the time the value of these heritage buildings....
There was tremendous loss in the 1960s and 1970s of very good fine old
buildings. The Birks building was just a wonderful, flamboyant high Victorian
structure that stood at the head of Gore Park, and (old) City Hall. Those were
the two major losses of the landmark buildings in the downtown.*

—Nina Chappel

*There was the old Birks building and some people thought it was glorious. I
thought it was as ugly as sin. The old City Hall was a dreadful building. It
was built in a different time when money didn't matter and efficiency and
effectiveness didn't matter and when taxes were a pittance.*

—Jack MacDonald

Hamilton Harbour with the steel mills in the background.

The Consensus

Although some today feel the downtown urban renewal project was
a mistake, this was not the case in the '50s and '60s. At that time,
there was a general consensus that something had to be done. By
the late 1950s and early '60s, the deterioration downtown had set in
to such an extent that stores were sitting vacant, movie theatres had
emptied, and even the market was losing business. The once
jammed, noisy, downtown streets that had so much life and vitality
were showing clear signs of decay. People were simply not coming

downtown in the numbers that they once had, and it was generally agreed that something dramatic had to be done to attract them once again.

Unfortunately, what was ignored was the reason why the downtown was losing its vitality. By 1960, most families had cars. A shift of people to the suburbs on the mountain and other neighbourhoods on the outskirts of the city had already occurred. A number of shopping centres, such as the Limeridge and Eastgate Malls, had either been built or were being planned; these malls had free parking and were much more convenient to suburbanites than was the downtown.

Hamilton was also a city where most people worked in manufacturing. The demand was low for downtown office space to

View of Dundas from the escarpment, with Hamilton in the background.

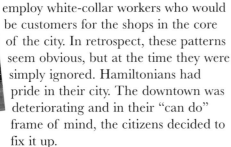
The Vasco da Gama Hall, a Portugese community centre on James St. North.

employ white-collar workers who would be customers for the shops in the core of the city. In retrospect, these patterns seem obvious, but at the time they were simply ignored. Hamiltonians had pride in their city. The downtown was deteriorating and in their "can do" frame of mind, the citizens decided to fix it up.

Mayor Lloyd D. Jackson, who was in office from 1950 to 1962, is credited

with the first efforts to fix up the downtown, and his signature project was the new city hall. The old city hall on James Street North had been built in 1889. It was an elegant structure in French Romanesque style, built of Newcastle stone with graceful arches and a high clock tower. Jack MacDonald and others did not like the building, but many had nostalgic feelings for this structure that had been at the centre of civic life for such a long time. Jackson and his supporters not only wanted a more functional building to meet the needs of the growing city, but they felt that a new city hall would symbolize the spirit of Hamilton in this dynamic post-war era. What convinced others was that Eaton's wanted the land of the old city hall to expand their department store and it was felt that this would stimulate other development in the downtown. The old building and site was sold to Eaton's in 1955, for $800,000. It was later demolished.

When the city had assembled the land for the new city hall on Main Street West, Pigott Construction was given the contract to build the white marble-clad building.

On November 21st, 1960, to a fanfare of trumpets from the balcony of the council chamber, Governor-General Georges P. Vanier snipped the red ribbon that bound the glass wall of doors, and Hamilton's new civic administrative building became a reality.

—Marjorie Freeman Campbell[1]

Controversy was generated by the marble, which kept falling off the building, and the roof, which leaked. Ultimately, a judicial inquiry into the construction of the building was mounted. The inquiry was critical of Pigott and the city, but generally the new city hall was considered a successful first step in the rejuvenation of the downtown.

The second phase of downtown redevelopment was to be through urban renewal, and the chief proponent of this plan was Victor Copps, who was elected mayor in 1962.[2] The National

Buildings replaced by the Jackson Square shopping centre.

Hamilton City Hall as it looks today.

The Hamilton Art Gallery. INSET: *Statuary in the Irving Zucker Sculpture Court.*

were completely cleared. A high-rise apartment building was put up overlooking the harbour, and about 100 public housing town houses were built, as well as parks and two new schools. Then, in September 1964, City Council approved a study, by Murray V. Jones and Associates, of urban renewal for the core of the city. Six months later, Jones recommended the redevelopment of

Mayor Vic Copps wielding the wrecking ball at the start of demolition for the civic square project in 1968.

260 acres in the York Street area and a 44-acre site in the downtown, called Civic Square.

Housing Act was amended in 1954, to allow federal money to be used for urban renewal. This would be a federal, provincial, and municipal program: all three levels of government would participate in paying the costs of acquiring, clearing, and servicing the land in deteriorated areas of the city. The land would then be used either for municipal services such as parks and cultural buildings, or sold or leased to private interests. The city would then reap the benefits of both higher taxes on the land and rejuvenated neighbourhoods.

Hamilton's first urban renewal project was at Van Wagner's Beach, where houses were acquired and demolished to make way for a park. The next step was the more ambitious North End Project. A number of factories and deteriorated houses were acquired and demolished. Altogether, seven blocks, as well as scattered properties,

The Civic Square Project

Murray Jones had recommended that the city give priority to the York Street project because he found serious deterioration in the area, but the city politicians chose to focus on Civic Square because they felt that this would be the catalyst to rejuvenating the downtown. The 44 acres was a choice piece of property immediately north of the new city hall, stretching from Main Street to Merrick and from James to Bay Streets. It housed 260 businesses and 500 people in small, mostly three storey structures. Eighty-two per cent of the buildings had been built before 1900. Jones proposed an ambitious plan to completely clear the site and erect new civic buildings, including a theatre-auditorium,

For several years, vacant lots characterized the civic square project in downtown Hamilton.

levels of government, but with John Munro, the young Liberal cabinet minister from Hamilton East, smoothing out problems in Ottawa, things went well. Finally, on September 11, 1967, the deadline for submission of tenders to develop the 10.4 acres of commercial property in the square was reached, and two companies submitted bids: Triton Centres Limited, a major development company, and First Wentworth Development Company, a wholly owned subsidiary of Pigott Construction Company.

A review committee of forty people was set up to study the two bids. They found the Triton proposal superior on 8 out of 10 points, but the city politicians, led by Vic Copps and Jack MacDonald, awarded the contract to First Wentworth. Accusations were made

planetarium, education centre, library, farmers' market, art gallery, and trade and convention centre. Space was also to be made for a grand promenade and parks. Over 10 acres of the land was to be used for commercial purposes, which would include a shopping mall, hotel, and apartment buildings.

The response to the plan was enthusiastic. The *Spectator* called it "undoubtedly the most ambitious attempt to resurrect a city ever undertaken in Canada." Soon, the newspaper claimed, the downtown area would be ringed with apartment buildings "built to accommodate the people who will flock to the exciting new concept of living."[3] Others saw the scheme as a way to attract much needed private investment to the downtown.

It took two and a half years to get the approvals from different

that the process was unfair and biased in favour of the local company, but the decision had been made and nothing could be done about it. This was to be the beginning of a major controversy that polarized the city around the Civic Square Project for years.

The 260 merchants who were to be displaced by the massive urban renewal project had been told that they would have the "right of first refusal" to relocate in the new shopping mall that was to be built. It soon became

John Munro on the campaign trail in the 1960s.

apparent that most of these businesses were not appropriate for this upscale development and few could afford the new rents. Many were unhappy, but there was nothing that they could do. A large number of the merchants were unable to relocate and simply disappeared.

There were difficulties in the negotiations between First Wentworth and the city from the start. Joseph Pigott Junior led the negotiations for the development company and many found him demanding and arrogant. He had little time for the city hall staff assigned to work on the project and soon Vic Copps and Jack MacDonald became the city negotiating committee. Even they had difficulty dealing with the constantly changing demands of Pigott.

The First Wentworth plan was considerably different from the original, and Murray Jones was engaged to work with them to revise it. Six months after the contract was awarded, Joseph Pigott

Some areas of the downtown are being renovated and restored, such as these old stone rowhouses on James St. South, which have been converted into shops.

The new Hamilton Public Library is part of the Jackson Square project.

announced that the developers would need an extra 100,000 square feet, increasing the commercial part of the square from 10 to 18 acres. The extra land would be taken from the land set aside for public buildings. After a closed door meeting, Council passed this revision. Murray Jones was sent back to the drawing board to revise the plan yet again.

The public was now beginning to become alarmed by what they saw was happening in the square and by the one sided negotiations in which Pigott seemed to get everything he asked for. The demolitions began in 1968 and 1969, and yet nothing seemed to be settled as to where the buildings should be located. To make matters worse, virtually all of the discussions were going on behind closed doors. Marvin Wasserman, president of the Hamilton

Copps Coliseum was named for the popular mayor Vic Copps.

architects to criticize the plan. But despite the opposition, Council passed the latest revised plan. The SOS committee appealed this decision to the Ontario Municipal Board. Herman Turkstra, acting as the lawyer for the group, did a masterful job exposing the inadequacy of the plans, but in the end the OMB refused to overturn the decision of Council.

City Council had done its best to accommodate the demands of First Wentworth, but the developers' plan had fundamental problems. The very day after the OMB completed its hearings, the development company was granted its fourth extension. Some members of council were furious and thought they had been misled. The rumour was that First Wentworth was having difficulty arranging the financing, but the mayor and Jack MacDonald were able to hold the support of the majority of Council. Gradually, in the following months, the power of First Wentworth faded. In the end, the financial analysts did what the politicians found so difficult—they refused to finance the project and it

Downtown Association, complained that the original concept of Civic Square as a meeting place had been jeopardized.

> *The plan was presented three and a half years ago but nothing has been finalized.... It is time that the game of hopscotch with the market, library, theatre-auditorium and art gallery come to a stop.*
> —*The Spectator*, April 2, 1969

Mrs. Sheila Zack, the wife of a well-known merchant, began to organize an opposition group that called itself Save Our Square (SOS). They created the largest political protest dealing with city issues that has ever been seen in the city. SOS took out full-page advertising in *The Spectator*, describing their position, and distributed leaflets and bumper stickers. They also brought together lawyers and

The Farmers' Market, a longtime feature of Hamilton's downtown, is now a part of Jackson Square.

collapsed. Finally, on March 2, 1970, the majority of Council voted to terminate the contract with First Wentworth.

The city was in deep trouble. Acres of prime downtown land had been demolished and had been sitting vacant for over a year, and the public was in an uproar over the city's handling of what was the most important contract in its history. But then, as if heaven-sent, Yale Properties Limited appeared, promising to develop the 18 acres of land. Even more promising was their firm financing through Standard Life Assurance Company.

The difficulties were still not over, however. The project had to be redesigned yet again, and the public buildings were again moved about like chess pieces. The long promised second department store for the mall vanished. The apartment complex was cancelled and then the hotel disappeared. The controversy had been going on

With his classical guitar, Jerry Moore entertains outside Jackson Square. INSET: *A woman relaxes in the Jackson Square roof garden.*

for so long now that virtually all of the major players were losing confidence in the city redevelopment project and in turn they were losing confidence in the economic viability of Hamilton's downtown. As late as the early 1980s, acres of demolished property were still sitting vacant on the Civic Square site.

It ultimately took government involvement to finish the square. The city built Copps Coliseum at the corner of Bay and Merrick, and on July 20, 1978, the Ontario government announced that it would build a $35 million trade and convention centre and a provincial office tower in the square. The politicians were ecstatic:

Once word gets out that the centre is a GO, I think you will see them (hotels) running to us. We can offer them a pretty damn attractive location at Bay and King Streets connected to a new art gallery, theatre-auditorium, shopping, a library-market and a convention centre.

—Controller Ian Stout

Others, like alderman Pat Ford, believed the centre "could be the catalyst to attract two or three hotels to the area."[4] Civic pride and boosterism was still alive in Hamilton.

Despite all of the controversy over the project, the city has benefitted from a number of public buildings like the theatre-auditorium, convention centre and art gallery. The new library with the farmers' market is well used, and Copps Coliseum is busy with hockey, rock concerts and special events. An elegant hotel also graces the commercial section of Lloyd D. Jackson Square. But years after it was completed, the massive urban redevelopment program remains controversial. Jack MacDonald, the former long-time city politician and mayor, continues to defend it as the project that halted the decay of the downtown. Others are scathing in their criticism, claiming that the project speeded deterioration. "We did all the wrong things in Hamilton," David Coming, a planner in private practice, said recently. "What did we learn? We learned that mega-projects don't solve downtown problems."[5]

A sunset panorama of Hamilton's East End, from the escarpment.

A view of the North End of the city from the harbour. The RHYC is visible on the shoreline.

The Hamilton Harbour Controversy

A second controversy in the 1970s developed around Hamilton Harbour, which did not create the furor that downtown redevelopment did, but its impact has lasted longer. The bay has always been a place of both recreation and commerce. After the canal was cut through the Beach Strip in the 1820s, Hamilton became an important port bringing passengers and raw materials for industry and exporting agricultural and industrial products. But the bay has also been an important centre of recreation. Sailing has always been popular on the bay in the summer, as have ice boating, skating, and, at one time, curling in winter. Boathouses lined the shore in the west end of the harbour, where people could rent canoes and rowboats. Steamer cruises left the James Street dock to tour the harbour and lake, and many remember dancing the night away on romantic midnight cruises to Port Dalhousie and Toronto.

Up until the 1920s, the bay was used even more than it is today. Swimming spots dotted the full length of the city shore. People fished and caught turtles in the summer, and many had huts for ice fishing in the winter. Ice-cutting companies gave employment in February and March to numbers of seasonal workers. The ice was stored in sheds along the waterfront and sold to households through the summer months for refrigeration. But all of this changed in the

1920s when pollution of the water closed the swimming areas, stopped the fishing, and halted the ice-cutting business. At the same time, the radial trains and automobiles gave people greater mobility, so they were able to find other recreation. But people were still nostalgic for the time when the bay was the centre of much of what people enjoyed about Hamilton.

In 1912, the federal government passed the Hamilton Harbour Commissioners Act, which created a three-member body to oversee the development of the harbour. Over the years, new docking facilities were built to facilitate commercial shipping, and large-scale landfill projects in the harbour were approved. By far the biggest of these projects was in the east end of the bay, and both Stelco and Dofasco were the chief beneficiaries of the

The Cargo Master *was a dredge in Hamilton Harbour. For decades, controversy swirled around the Hamilton Harbour and its operations.*

policy. It was a great deal for the steel companies. They could fill the water with slag, a waste product of the steel making process that had to be disposed of, and at the same time create land that they could use to expand their plant and docking facilities for the freighters that brought in the iron ore.

Not much discussion about the landfill practices took place until the filling began in the west end of the harbour. It had become tacitly

accepted that the east end of the harbour was devoted to industry and the west end would remain for recreation, but in 1957 the Harbour Commissioners sold water lots to an American company for a scrap metal yard. In time, this company sold its interests in the water lots to the Lax Brothers, who were Hamilton scrap metal dealers. In 1968, the Lax Brothers announced that they were going to fill in some 50 acres of water lots just off Bay Street near the railway yards in the

This view from Coote's Paradise shows both the High Level Bridge and the 403. The bridges span the defunct Desjardins Canal.

A Great Lakes freighter unloads iron ore pellets at Stelco. Hamilton remains one of the busiest ports on the Great Lakes.

west end of the bay and build a multi-million dollar residential development called Bayshore Village. The trucks began arriving that summer, and the fill began despite the fact that no approvals had ever been given by the city.

Suddenly, the controversy over the filling of the bay was a full-blown issue in Hamilton. It was shown that through the policies of the Harbour Commissioners hundreds of acres of the bay had been filled and approximately one-third of the actual surface of the bay had disappeared. Virtually all of these decisions had been made behind closed doors with little or no public discussion. Environmentalists and community activists were outraged. Bill Powell, the Chair of the Hamilton Conservation Authority, went on the attack. He attempted to stop the steel companies from acquiring a further 328 acres of water lots in 1972. When this attempt was blocked by the Ontario government, he lashed out. "I'll bet the lobbyists from the two steel companies were just about camping down there (at Queen's Park).... I can smell the whole situation from here."[6]

The controversy took an unexpected turn when some members of City Council tried to remove the city appointee to the Harbour Commission, Kenneth Elliott. About six months later, Elliott was arrested on 11 counts of fraud, bribery, forgery, conspiracy, and breach of trust for his part in a scandal around the awarding of dredging contracts. He was ultimately convicted and sentenced to six years in prison. This was heady stuff indeed. Hamilton and its harbour were in the midst of one of the messiest Canadian political scandals in the post-war era.

What all of this controversy and scandal ultimately did was draw attention back to the bay. Many people came to realize that in the rush to bring industry and build the city, one of the greatest assets of the community, Hamilton Harbour, had been drastically reduced in size and polluted to the point where scientists called it "an 11 square mile sewer."[7] There was even concern that the water might have lost its ability to rejuvenate itself. The wrenching process led to a rededication to rehabilitate the bay by improving water quality, providing greater public access, and bringing the bay back to its original function as one of the major recreational facilities of the city.

Some of this has been accomplished. The Lax Brothers never developed their property. It was purchased and became the Bayfront Park. An even more dramatic development has been the waterfront trail

from Princess Point to the North End. To further this process, a new agreement was reached between the city and the federal government, in which much of the land in the west end of the harbour will be turned over to the city, a new $10 million marine museum will be built on the harbour, and the waterfront trail will be extended. Sheila Copps, cabinet minister and federal Member of Parliament for Hamilton East, called it "The most important development for the city in decades." Others saw it as the beginning of the reorientation of the city back towards the water:

This [Hamilton deal] is symptomatic of what is happening in North America and Europe. The public is now facing the water, instead of turning its back to it.

—Beth Benson, Executive Director,
Waterfront Regeneration Trust

Economic Realignments

In the 1960s and '70s, Hamilton's economy was strong. The two steel companies were doing particularly well. They had close to 30,000 employees between them, and profits were strong. Dofasco was the smaller and more aggressive of the two. They were a non-union company, but they paid union wages, had a profit-sharing plan, and viewed themselves as a family-run company. The Sherman family, who founded Dofasco, lived in Hamilton and sponsored sports teams and a company choir, and every year put on what they described as "the world's largest Christmas party" for their employees and their families.

Stelco was unionized, but relations between workers and management had improved significantly since the days of the bitter 1946 strike. A strike had occurred in 1958, a wildcat strike in 1966, and again a strike in 1969, but generally the day-to-day relationships were cordial and Stelco workers had pride in their company. It came as a complete shock in 1968 when Stelco announced that its head office was moving to Toronto and the company was going to build another primary steel making facility at Nanticoke on Lake Erie. The one

The Bruce Trail

In 1960, Raymond Lowes, a Hamiltonian and a metallurgist with Stelco, proposed the idea of a walking trail along the brow of the Niagara Escarpment from Queenston, on the Niagara River, through Hamilton, the Dundas Valley, and all the way to Tobermory on the Bruce Peninsula, for a total of 740 kilometres

in length. In March 1963, the trail was incorporated, and was completed by volunteer labour four years later in 1967. The Niagara Escarpment was named a World Biosphere Reserve by the United Nations in 1990.

McMaster University Medical Centre. INSET: *Convocation Hall passageway at McMaster University.*

concession that was made to Hamilton was to move a number of middle management white-collar staff into an office building in the new Jackson Square complex that was in the planning stages at that time. This is what Hamilton's federal cabinet minister, John Munro, said about the issue in a telegram:

I'm damn mad…. This city has been more than fair to Stelco over the years. The men of Hamilton have devoted a good portion of their lives in making the company as prosperous as it is today…. Hamilton is apparently good enough to sweat for Stelco but not good enough for anything else.

—*The Spectator*, November 1, 1968

This announcement shook the confidence of the leaders of Hamilton. Other companies had moved out of the city: Carr Fastener had moved to Stoney Creek, and A.H. Tallman and Wallace-Barnes had moved to Burlington. Even more serious, the Studebaker car assembly plant had closed down in 1966, throwing close to 800 out of work. Was this an indication of the future?

And yet other parts of the city continued to expand and prosper. McMaster was growing, and with the addition of the new medical school it extended its reach into the hospitals across the city. The establishment of the medical school/hospital complex in Westdale again caused major controversy. The school was to block King Street,

The Sunken Gardens, shown in this old postcard, were replaced by the medical school.

apprenticeships, and contract training in a wide variety of areas, on both a full-time and part-time basis. From its inception, Mohawk was one of the largest colleges in the province and had an enviable reputation. Maclean's Guide to Colleges recently wrote: "Flourishing within Ontario's industrial heartland, Mohawk College has become a leader among Canadian colleges."

Daisies in Gore Park.

It is interesting that Mohawk College is located on the mountain and McMaster is in the west end of the city. The draw to the suburbs in Hamilton was very strong at the time that the college was established. The roads up the mountain, such as the Claremont Access and the Jolley Cut, were improved so that commuting became much easier. Not only were large numbers of people moving

which went through the west end of the city, demolish a number of homes, and eliminate the Sunken Gardens, a special park of the Royal Botanical Gardens. The controversy went on for some months, but in the end City Council voted to approve the medical school.

Another significant development was the establishment of Mohawk College in 1967. The origins of Mohawk go back to the founding of the Provincial Institute of Textiles in the mid 1940s, when textiles were the second largest industry in the city. In the late 1950s, the school became the Hamilton Institute of Technology (HIT), where a number of courses were taught in a wide variety of trades. When the provincial government established the Community College System, Mohawk was founded and the HIT was integrated into its structure. The new community college established a campus on Fennel Avenue. Soon it was offering diploma courses,

The Lilac Dell of the Royal Botanical Gardens.

St. John's Anglican Church in Ancaster.
INSET: *A modern suburb in Ancaster.*

to the mountain, but also new suburbs were springing up in Ancaster, Stoney Creek, Dundas, and Waterdown. Numbers of people who worked in Hamilton were now living as far away as Burlington. The excellent road system that had been built made it convenient to commute, but this suburbanization weakened the downtown and the older neighbourhoods under the mountain.

Greater mobility and a more regionally integrated economy were drawing people closer together, and old boundaries made less and less sense. The provincial government saw the need for greater co-ordination of municipalities, and on January 1, 1974, the Hamilton-Wentworth Regional Government was established, creating a two-tiered government of the six municipalities in the County of Wentworth. Anne Jones was appointed the first chair of the Regional Government.

High Brow and Low Brow

The reason why I live in Hamilton is that it's a pretence free zone. You know, life is hard enough being yourself; it's impossible when you're pretending to be somebody else, so I think that permeates the sense of humour too…. Where the rubber hits the road, that's where you'll find a Hamiltonian.

—Steve Smith (Red Green)

Burlington's Brant Inn was one of the most popular music and dancing spots in Southern Ontario.

Hamilton has always had a rough edge to it. It is after all a blue-collar town where most people earn their living by the honest sweat of their labours. As Steve Smith points out, this affects the way that people live their lives, their humour and their entertainment. As early as the 1920s and probably even before that time, the dance halls of the city were home to a new wildness. The vaudeville players preferred Hamilton to Toronto because people understood the off-colour jokes and the acts could be more than a touch risqué.

Music is at the centre of the Hamilton sensibility and it has always been the new music that has attracted the young people. In the swing era of the 1930s and '40s, Burlington's Brant Inn and the Flamingo Club in Hamilton were the hottest jazz spots in Ontario. Duke Ellington, Fats Waller, and Count Bassie all played in these venues, and local musicians made a good living playing in the clubs.

In the 1970s, Hamilton was a hotbed of rock 'n' roll. Teenage Head, an early punk group, was one of a string of prominent bands from Hamilton.

Honest to God you could see any kind of music in Hamilton. One night Dick Washington and I went out … and we saw Dizzie Gillespie out at the Westdale Tavern and then after he was through we went to the Flamingo and saw a fella called George Ald, a tenor man with Benny Goodman and different bands like that—and all in the same night in Hamilton here.

—Fred Puser[8]

When rock 'n' roll came on the scene in the 1950s, young fans could barely contain their enthusiasm. The first concert was held in the Hamilton Forum in the spring of 1958, with an audience of 4,000 excited young people. On the bill were Frankie Avalon, the Monotones, Ottawa's 16-year-old Paul Anka, and a number of other singers and groups. Although the older generation feared that a riot might break out, Fred Marshall, a *Spectator* reporter who was sent to cover the event, thought that the fans were reasonably well behaved.

While the excited patrons jumped to the abandoned playing and remarkable contortions of the Royal Teens of "Short Shorts" fame, they sank back in relaxed ecstasy to hear of the ballads of George Hamilton IV.

—The Spectator, April 17, 1958

Soon Hamiltonians were playing and creating their own rock and roll. In 1961, Jack Wilkinson, who ran a local theatrical agency, estimated that there were at least four or five hundred young rock 'n' roll musicians in the city.

The young musicians will play in basements or bedrooms, approaching their work with an intensity Beethoven might have taken towards his Ninth. They'll carry a tune throughout the day, humming into workmates ears. Work for them is often a nagging pause between sessions.

—The Spectator, March 23, 1961

Jay, a young singer with a group called the Monarchs, said that the quality of the musicians was great. "The proof is that some of us are good enough to get paid for playing. We can get $100 a night, two nights a week." Older people thought the music was "weird" and others, like Ernest Hutton, the principal of Hill Park Secondary School, believed "rock 'n' roll is a fad the youngsters grow out of when they reach 16," but popular

The Grange Tavern, a popular music venue, was demolished for the Civic Square Project.

music was here to stay. Hamilton produced musical groups like Crowbar that became well known across Canada.

One musician who landed in Hamilton in about 1959 was Conway Twitty. While he was here, he wrote "It's Only Make Believe," one of the classic tunes of the era. He ended up heading back to the United States, but another musician from the American south who did settle in Canada was Ronnie Hawkins, who played a lot in Hamilton. Hawkins sang rock a billy, and in the 1960s and into the '70s he would play at clubs like the Golden Rail and the Grange. On nights when Hawkins was playing and the club was packed with young workers, some coming straight from their shift, the excitement of the music and the crowd would make the whole place vibrate.

In those days, Ronnie Hawkins played with a group called "The Hawks," who were all young musicians from Southern Ontario working out of Hamilton. The Hawks went on to be known simply as "The Band," one of the most sophisticated and successful musical groups

Hamilton Place, the city's home for large cultural events.

of the 1970s. They played an innovative electronic music that was a mixture of country and rock and was loved by the fans who packed the Hamilton clubs when they were first starting out. There are people in the city who still remember Robbie Robertson, the best-known member of The Band, as a sixteen-years-old playing with Ronnie Hawkins and the Hawks. He was so young looking that he was told to wear sunglasses, and as soon as a set was over he had to get out of the bar because he was underage.

Another popular musician who lived in Dundas at this time was Stan Rogers. Stan came from a Nova Scotian family, but he was born and raised in Hamilton. He was a singer/songwriter who played in the folk music tradition. "A big man—six foot four—built like a fire

truck and [he] possessed a voice that rumbled from his toes. He could bluff and bellow yet was at heart a poet and intellect."[9] Tragically, Stan Rogers was killed in an airplane accident at the height of his career, in June of 1983.

Hamilton was filled with music in this period. Boris Brott became the conductor of the Hamilton Philharmonic Orchestra (HPO) in 1969, and brought to it his flare for music and his unfailing instincts for promoting the orchestra. Brott had trained with Leonard Bernstein and had been a founder of the Canadian Brass; when he came to Hamilton, he was Canada's youngest conductor. He transformed the HPO into a professional orchestra with a core of thirty full-time, resident musicians. The orchestra played sold-out concerts in Hamilton and toured across

Johnny Papalia

Organized crime has long been a feature of Hamilton life. Rocco Perri and members of his gang were folk heroes of a sort because few people in the city supported prohibition and everyone seemed to know someone who was a bootlegger, but the new group of men who took over organized crime after Perri disappeared have come to be seen as much more sinister.

Johnny Papalia, or Johnny Pops as he was known on the street, was at the centre of organized crime in Hamilton and Ontario for many years. His father, Anthony, was a member of Perri's gang and he raised his family of six boys and one girl on Railway Street. Johnny became a professional criminal as early as the 1940s. He spent an apprenticeship period in Montreal in the early 1950s, working with the Galente Organization, a Mafia family. In 1955, he returned to Hamilton and went into gambling, loan sharking, extortion, and the smuggling of narcotics. He was involved in the notorious 1961 beating of the gambler Max Bluestein in Toronto's Town Tavern.

At the height of his career, in 1961, Papalia was arrested in the United States on a charge of conspiring to import $150 million worth of heroin. His connections with both the Montreal and Buffalo Mafia families made him a vital link in the heroin trade that brought drugs from Turkey through Italy, France, Canada, and into the United States. (This was the so-called "French Connection.") Papalia was ultimately convicted of this crime and sentenced to 10 years in prison in the United States. He was released by the New York Parole Board after serving only five years of his sentence on grounds that he was suffering from advanced tuberculosis. After he got back to Hamilton he made a "miraculous" recovery.

Over succeeding decades, Papalia continued his organized crime activities. He was frequently named by law enforcement officers and the media as a major Canadian Mafia figure, but he was not convicted of a major crime. He continued to live in Hamilton and to use his company, Monarch Vending Machines, on Railway Street, as a front for his criminal operations. Then, on May 30, 1997, he was killed, execution-style, with a bullet to the head in the parking lot of the vending machine company. A man by the name of Ken Murdock later admitted to being the hit man, and it was alleged that two brothers, Pat and Angelo Musitano, had ordered the killing. In the trial, the Musitano brothers were convicted of conspiring to murder Carmen Barilaro, one of Papalia's lieutenants, but acquitted of the Papalia killing.[10]

Canada to high critical acclaim. Brott was an innovator. He staged a concert with the Hamilton pop group "Tranquility Base" and established children's concerts and a pop series. He even took the orchestra into the Dofasco steel mills for a concert. But perhaps the greatest indication of Brott's success was that he increased the Hamilton audiences for the orchestra from 23,000 to 225,000.

Energy and controversy infused Hamilton's cultural sector in the 1970s. A major pornography trial took place, involving people who went on to be successful figures in the entertainment industry. A group of students established the McMaster Film Society and made a number of films of varying quality. In the summer of 1970, a group shot a film called *The Columbus of Sex*, which featured nudity and explicit scenes. Some of the film was shot in the backyard of George Grant, one of McMaster's most prestigious scholars. The night the film was to be shown for the first time, the audience gathered in one of the theatres of the arts buildings at the university. One person who attended is still amazed by what happened.

We were watching the film when suddenly these big burly guys rushed in, turned on the lights, ordered the film to stop and told us that we were all to leave immediately. It was the police, if you can imagine, and they were saying that the film was pornographic.

—Marsha Hewitt

To the credit of the people who where involved in *The Columbus of Sex*, they decided that they were going to fight the charge. In the ensuing trial in Hamilton's courthouse, they gathered some of the leading intellectuals and art critics in the country to testify on their behalf, but despite their efforts they were convicted. It is interesting to look back to see who was involved in the McMaster Film Society. Ivan Reitman was the director of *The Columbus of Sex*. He went on to Hollywood, where he produced such films as *Animal House*, *Ghostbusters* and *Home Alone*. Others include Eugene Levy, Dave Thomas and Martin Short, who starred in SC-TV, and were all Hamilton boys.

Hamilton was on a roll in the 1960s and '70s. The steel mills were booming, and McMaster and Mohawk were growing to become centres of academic excellence. Professional theatre had arrived with Theatre Aquarius, and even the beloved Tiger Cats were at the top of their form. Ralph Sazio had put together a team that included such outstanding players as Angelo Mosca, Garney Henley, and a bevy of other great players. Hamilton was a town with pride.

The Canadian Brass entertain workers in the Dofasco steel mills.

Chapter Nine

REDISCOVERING THE CITY
(1980 – 2000 and Beyond)

In 1900, there was the sense that Hamilton, with its booming industries, rapidly growing population, and increasing wealth, could challenge Toronto and Montreal for the economic leadership of Ontario and Canada.

The anger over the move of Stelco's head office to Toronto in 1968 reflected the feeling that this local corporate giant had betrayed Hamilton's lingering dream of achieving metropolis status.

By the year 2000, Hamiltonians had set for themselves the more modest goal of becoming a livable city with a rich history, a diversity of cultures, and amenities within the larger urban concentration at the west end of Lake Ontario.

Hamilton's skyline at night. INSET: *Hess Village.*

Economic Erosion

The erosion of Hamilton's manufacturing sector was slow in developing. In the period after the Second World War, the textile and clothing industries found it impossible to compete against cheap imports from low-wage countries. Before the end of the '50s most of the companies of the city's second largest industry had closed up and quietly disappeared. When Studebaker shut its doors in 1966, a shock went through the city, but the auto industry had never been at the core of the city's economy.

Hamilton's industries had been created in the days after the National Policy of high tariffs, which gave Canadian companies an advantage when selling in the Canadian market. In the years immediately after the creation of NAFTA in the 1980s, many companies found it difficult to compete with American imports. But there was another reason for the shrinkage. Companies were diversifying into smaller, more economical units, and they closed big operations in centres such as Hamilton. The plant closures read like a "Who's Who" of Hamilton companies: Hoover in 1966, Slater Steel in the late 1960s, Coca Cola in the early 1980s, Otis Elevator in 1987, Firestone in 1988, Brown and Boggs in the early 1990s, Consumers Glass in 1997, International Harvester in 1999.

Even the steel companies, the largest manufacturing employers in the city, have gone through major restructuring. In the early 1980s,

Siemens Westinghouse on Burlington St., and (below) International Harvester on Hillyard St., sit vacant.

more than 30,000 worked in the steel mills. By the year 2001, Stelco employed 7,800 in Hamilton, and Dofasco's entire workforce had shrunk to 7,200. The demand for steel was down mainly because of the challenge of inexpensive plastics and competition from offshore steel producers. In 2000 it was estimated that foreign-made steel took up more than 44 per cent of the Canadian steel market.[1] Productivity per employee had improved as a result of changes in manufacturing processes and new machinery. The Hamilton steel companies are considered to be among the most innovative in the world, but the high growth of sales has disappeared and the companies will have to remain efficient to be profitable.

In the fifteen years from 1981 to 1996, manufacturing jobs in Hamilton shrank from 63,030 to 32,030,[2] but surprisingly this economic restructuring has not created much of a panic. As the number manufacturing jobs contracted, the service sector has grown. The largest employer in the city is now Hamilton Health Sciences Corporation (hospital services), with over 9,000 employees. The school board employs almost 6,000, and McMaster has 3,500 employees and roughly 15,000 students. The unemployment rate remains around 5 or 6 per cent, approximately the same rate as Toronto and other centres in the area.

What has been happening is that the Hamilton economy and its workforce have become more and more integrated with Toronto and the Greater Toronto Area (GTA) on the north side of Lake Ontario, and St. Catharines and the Niagara Peninsula on the south side. A study found that in 1980, 6,500 commuters entered the Hamilton region every day. By 1995, that number was reversed: 6,500 more people commuted out of the region than came in.[3] Manufacturing is also becoming more diversified. Small firms are springing up along the major transportation

corridors like the QEW in Stoney Creek and Burlington, and the 403 highway. The city has evolved from a one industry "Steeltown" into a more diversified city, integrated with the rapidly increasing urban concentration at the western end of Lake Ontario.

The City Above and Below the Mountain

The impact that these economic changes has made on Hamilton has been remarkable. The city has continued to grow but at a rate that is slower than any other metropolitan area in Ontario other than Thunder Bay. However, the differences in the growth rates within the city's areas are striking. The numbers living on the mountain have been increasing rapidly, but the lower city has been stagnant or even shrinking.[4]

Morning light on Hamilton's skyline.

This sculpture at the old James St. train station commemorates the many immigrants who made Hamilton their home.

	Hamilton Mountain	Lower City	City of Hamilton
1956	50,877	200,037	250,914
1976	109,960	202,045	312,005
1996	137,234	185,118	322,352

It is almost as if two cities have developed in Hamilton. The mountain is a city of suburbs and shopping malls where most people get around by car. The area contains some apartments, but 63.6 per cent of the homes are detached houses. The household income of people on the mountain is 30.7 per cent higher than that in the rest of the city and only 30.4 per cent are tenants. Most of the growth continues south of Mohawk Road. If these patterns continue, it is likely the mountain will soon overtake the lower city in population.

The lower city, by contrast, has much older housing stock. Many of the neighbourhoods close to the centre of the city were built in the nineteenth century. A much higher percentage of the people living in the lower city live in apartments, at 42.8 per cent. In the downtown, many stores are sitting vacant and the office vacancy rate hovers at around 20 per cent. Despite these conditions, 78 per cent of all of the jobs in Hamilton are located in the lower city.

Hamilton continues to have many attractive features. Immigration remains high, and in 1999, almost 25 per cent of the population was born outside the country. The crime rate is lower than in the rest of the country, and perhaps the most striking aspect is Hamilton's affordability. While residents in the City of Toronto and almost every other area of the Greater Toronto Area, struggle with the high cost of housing and property taxes, Hamilton residents enjoy much lower house prices and a number of apartments are available at reasonable rental costs. In the 1990s, for the first time, people in Toronto began moving to Hamilton, to take advantage of affordable housing.

A renovated Victorian home on Park St. in Dundas

The New Hamilton

When the Harris provincial government announced its intention to restructure the Hamilton-Wentworth Region into one municipal government the reaction was predictable. The people in the City of Hamilton largely supported the move, but many residents in the surrounding area of the old Wentworth County were outraged. Part of the reason for the opposition to restructuring was that residents in the county felt their history, traditions, and identity would be swallowed up in the larger city. These residents also perceived that Hamilton's lower city and particularly the downtown were in economic decline and that residents of the surrounding area would be saddled with higher taxes to deal with these problems.

The opposition to restructuring was intense. A *Spectator*-sponsored survey found that 78 per cent of the residents of Dundas and 74.8 per cent of from Flamborough were opposed to restructuring. As the controversy developed various compromises were attempted, but opinions only hardened. Toni Skarica, the Conservative Member of Provincial Parliament for Wentworth North (later called Wentworth-Burlington) felt that he had a commitment from Premier Mike Harris that restructuring would not be imposed. When the government moved ahead anyway, and on December 21, 1999, the restructuring bill became law, he resigned his seat in the legislature in protest. In the ensuing by-election, the Liberal candidate, Ted McMeekin, the Flamborough Mayor, was elected by a landslide. The message to the government could not be clearer. The voters of Wentworth North wanted nothing to do with restructuring. The difficulty was that whether they wanted it or not the legislation had been passed and they were going to be part of the new city of Hamilton.

The old stone building in Waterdown that used to be Weeks Hardware. All of the old Region of Hamilton/Wentworth is now part of the "new" City of Hamilton.

The November 2000 election was not only the first municipal election in the new millennium, but it was the first election in the "new" Hamilton, including all of the old municipalities of Wentworth: Ancaster, Dundas, Flamborough, Glanbrook, Hamilton, and Stoney Creek. The new city is a diverse area of 468,000 people that includes farms, light and heavy industry, and extensive services such as hospitals and post-secondary educational institutions.

The outcome of the election was a surprise. It had been predicted that Bob Morrow, the longest serving mayor in Hamilton's history, would easily win, but Bob Wade, the mayor of Ancaster, one of the smallest towns in the new city, was elected. He started his term with a frank assessment of the problems facing the new city.

Modern roads and automobiles have made the suburbs accessible to large numbers of people.

Bob Morrow, the longest-serving mayor of the City of Hamilton, was the last mayor of the "old" city.

During the municipal election I said that it was time for leaders in this city to start telling the hard truths, and the truth is that Hamilton's economy has fallen behind. If Ontario is at a crucial juncture in its history, so definitely is Hamilton.

—Mayor Bob Wade,
February 13, 2001

But the mayor is far from pessimistic about the future of the city. He is working to implement his economic strategy that includes "smart growth," a trade corridor from Ontario to Western New York State, in which Hamilton will play a key role.

We're into a new millennium. We can make a start as a brand new city. We have an opportunity, I believe, to make this city one of the greatest cities in Canada…. I want Hamilton to be a welcoming city, a comfortable city for people to live in, and a city where people continue to raise their families and continue their careers.

—Mayor Bob Wade, January 2001[5]

The New City of Hamilton has many advantages over other centres. It has a strong tax base with a mature economy that has both large, stable manufacturing companies and new industries. It has a solid infrastructure of roads, railways and an airport, and its hospitals and educational institutions are among the best in Canada. The problems of deterioration in the downtown core remain, but even this issue is being addressed in a more realistic way.

A consensus now exists that mega projects do not solve the problems of the inner city, and the new solutions that are proposed encourage small, incremental steps. The key is to bring more people downtown so that this area can become a more livable and safer neighbourhood. This process has already begun. The elaborately decorated Pigott Building on James Street has been renovated into condominiums. The Labourers' International Union bought the old CNR station on James Street North, where so many immigrants first arrived in the city, and have converted it into a 50,000 square foot convention and banquet facility with office space on the second floor. The Royal Connaught Hotel is being renovated into a 150-room hotel with a 58-unit residential wing. The old *Spectator* building overlooking Gore Park is

The Piggott Building on James St. South, as reflected in a modern office tower.

Bob Wade, formerly the mayor of Ancaster, was elected the first mayor of the "new" city.

being converted into a 52-unit condominium. Recently it was announced that McMaster University would take over the courthouse on Main Street for 10 years to relieve the university's overcrowding problem.

All of these projects recognize the inherent value of the historical part of the city and its buildings and are renovating or using old buildings in the downtown. As people walk through Gore Park, few

Stained glass in the art deco Piggott Building on James St. South, the city's first skyscraper. The building was recently converted into condominiums.

The Gore Park Fountain

It is in Gore Park, the old centre of Hamilton, that the new city is being reborn and the story of the Gore Park Fountain is symbolic of that rebirth. In the late 1850s, Hamiltonians felt their town of 25,000 people was at the brink of greatness. The Great Western Railway had arrived in 1854 and in 1859 the new city water system was finally completed. On the sunny afternoon of June 3, 1859 a ceremony was held to

The Luna Station is the old CNR train station on James St. North. It was recently converted into a convention and banquet facility by the Labourers' International Union.

realize that surrounding them are buildings that date back to the 1840s. These are some of the oldest buildings in the core of any city in Ontario. They are the greatest assets of downtown Hamilton, and the renovation movement that has begun recognizes that they must be saved and enhanced. This process of renovation and preservation opens exciting possibilities for the city that sees its past as an asset of the future.

The city's main post office has recently been converted into the John Sopinka Courthouse. It sits across the street from the site of Hamilton's first, log courthouse.

inaugurate the new water system. When the taps were turned on,

A glorious shout arose as the glittering water sprang upwards and young and old rejoiced in the beautiful spectacle. Both the hydrants were then called into requisition; and from nozzles of an inch and an eighth bore, streams were thrown across the wide street and over the buildings on either side.
—*Hamilton Times,* June 3, 1859

This accomplishment generated such excitement and pride that Hamiltonians immediately began to plan for something on an even grander scale to demonstrate that the city had unlimited quantities of inexpensive pure water available. It was proposed that the city build a fountain in the centre of Gore Park. A letter writer to the *Spectator* gave this opinion:

The Gore is the first place that the stranger or visitor meets with upon entering the city and it stands as a sort of index to the whole. Its proper beautification is therefore an object of the first importance to the city.
—*The Spectator,* July 21, 1859

In true Hamilton style, heated debates about the fountain arose, and in the end it was decided to go ahead with funds raised by private subscription. The land was graded by teams of

The original Gore Park fountain, with the Birk's building and incline railway in the background. Since the fountain was built in 1860, Gore Park has been the centre of the city.

Workers and the unemployed finding their leisure in Gore Park in 1924, with the fountain in the background.

horses donated by William Hendrie. James Gay, superintendent of the cemetery, planted grass and trees. John Freed donated flowers. Finally, the two-storey fountain with bowls that distributed falling water was installed and paid for by the Bank of British North America. The waters of the huge ornate fountain would continue to flow for nearly 100 years.[6] Later statues of Queen Victoria, Sir John A. Macdonald and the Cenotaph were added to the park, and each time the money was raised by private subscription.

Gore Park has remained the centre of the community since George Hamilton set it aside for public use. First, it was a wood market and a place where settlers on their way to the west in their prairie schooners could spend the night. Religious revival meetings were held here; the near riot between the Orange and Green factions was on these streets; temperance rallies were held here; political "soap boxers" harangued the crowds; the military recruiting leagues in both world wars set up booths in Gore Park, and after the wars the solemn ceremonies to commemorate the war dead have been held every year on November 11 at the Cenotaph.

Then, in the 1950s, with the deterioration of the downtown, it was felt that something had to happen to bring life back to Gore Park. The fountain was taken down, and over the next few years the place fell into neglect as various planners and architects tried to find a way to rejuvenate the centre of the city. But nothing seemed to work. Then, in the 1980s, an even bolder plan was developed. A crew of city workers armed with chainsaws and jackhammers descended on

A mother and son share a moment beside the restored Gore fountain.

Looking down from the High Level Bridge to the Waterfront Trail. The trail's development symbolizes how Hamiltonians are reclaiming their waterfront.

the park with orders from the city. Within a few hours, century-old trees were felled and stone cobblestones were ripped up. All that was left standing were the Cenotaph and the forlorn statues of Sir John A. Macdonald and Queen Victoria at opposite ends of the park.

The city erupted.[7] Few events have polarized the people of Hamilton more than the destruction of Gore Park. The politicians speechified about it; the civil servants tried to explain; but nothing would mollify the public. Their park had been destroyed and they wanted it put back together again. Fortunately, the end of the story is

a happy one. The park was restored, and in fact restored to its former glory with an exact replica of the original fountain built in 1860. The work was completed for Hamilton's Sesquicentennial celebrations in 1996.

Today, Gore Park still has its odd triangular shape just as when it was first created by George Hamilton so many years ago. Surrounding the park on King Street are buildings, some dating as early as the 1840s and 1850s. The graceful nineteenth-century fountain showers its steady stream of water out of its bowls. Queen

Victoria, John A. Macdonald, and the Cenotaph, all images that hold special meaning for Hamiltonians, are there. Now the park is filled with trees, plants, and people, always lots of people. Gore Park and its fountain are symbols of Hamilton's history and it is here that the new city is being reborn.

Towards the New City

For decades, Hamilton was known for its heavy industry. As this image fades in relative importance, new prospects are appearing. There is much to be optimistic about in the future of the new City of Hamilton. The city's greatest asset has always been its location at the western end of Lake Ontario. The entire Golden Horseshoe area is booming and Hamilton is growing along with it.

But the city has other assets that are as important as its economy. Hamilton has the most spectacular location of any city in southern Ontario. The bay and the escarpment have long been a joy to the residents of the city. Now people are coming to understand that they have a wonderful resource in the rich history and culture of the city itself.

Lawn bowling in Gage Park.

ACKNOWLEDGEMENTS AND PHOTO CREDITS

The photographer wishes to thank: Dave Cage of the Stoney Creek Chamber of Commerce; Beth Nelmes and her son, Caleb; Jerry Moore; Ian Kerr-Wilson and the staff of the Hamilton Museum of Steam and Technology; Rick Zbucki, manager of cemeteries for the City of Hamilton; Bell Nesbitt, Fran Donnelly and the staff of Dundurn National Historic Site; and Mayor Bob Wade, City of Hamilton.

Photo Credits

Except for the following images, all photographs in this book were taken by Simon Wilson.

T = Top, B = Bottom, L = Left, R = Right, I = Inset

Archives of Ontario: 10B (RG2-344), 15 (F47-11-1-0-213); Art Gallery of Hamilton: 3 (with permission from Robert Hutchinson), 138 (with permission from the estate of Frank Panabaker), 143, 153 (with permission from Marjolaine Richardson); City of Toronto Archives: 44T, 51, 92T, 97 (SCC 244, Item 10.49), 100L(SCC 244, Item 95.43), 101I (SCC 244, Item 75.49), 121L(SCC 244, Item 42.30), 133R(SCC 244, Items 1.31 and 48.36), 150; Dundurn Castle, Bill Nesbit: 31B, 54; Reprinted with permission from *The Globe and Mail*: 174; Government of Ontario Art Collection: 11 (MGS-623328, with permission from the estate of C.W. Jefferys), 13 (MGS-623327, with permission from the estate of C.W. Jefferys), 16 (MGS-622610), 17 (MGS-622026), 18L, 18R (MGS-619857), 39; Hamilton Public Library: 9, 14, 21, 26, 27, 28, 29, 33, 36, 37T, 37B, 38, 41B; 45L, 47, 48, 50T, 53, 55, 56, 58, 59, 62, 63, 64, 65L, 65R, 66, 68, 69, 70, 71, 72, 73, 75, 76, 77, 79, 80, 82, 83, 84L, 84R, 85, 87L, 87R, 89, 91L, 94T, 94B, 95I, 96L, 96R, 99, 100R, 101T, 102, 103T, 104, 105L, 105R, 106, 107, 108T, 108B, 109T, 109I, 110, 111T, 111B, 112R, 113, 114L, 114R, 115, 116, 117T, 117B, 118, 119T, 119B, 120 (with permission from the estate of Frank Panabaker), 121R, 122T, 122B, 124L, 124R, 125, 126, 128T, 128L, 128R, 129T, 129B, 130L, 130R, 131L, 131R, 132, 133L, 134I, 135 (with permission from Robert Hutchinson), 136 (with permission from Robert Hutchinson), 139R, 140L, 140R, 141L, 141R (with permission from the estate of Frank Panabaker), 145L, 147, 148R, 151, 152, 154R, 158L, 159R, 160R, 169L, 171, 172L, 172R, 175, 181L, 185; Marsha Hewitt: 165; With Thanks to John Macaluso: 90; McMaster University Labour Studies Collection: 91R, 144, 146, 149L, 149R; Tom Moreman: 160L; National Archives of Canada: 10T, 20L, 30, 35 (with permission from the estate of C.W. Jefferys), 40, 57, 78, 88, 112, 123, 139L, 148L, 186L; National Gallery of Canada: 42; OWAHC: 92I, 93L, 93R, 103B, 127, 154L; Michael Quigley: 81; Walter Peace: 67; Westinghouse: 86.

Endnotes

Chapter 1
1. Marjorie Freeman Campbell, *A Mountain and a City* (Toronto: McClelland and Stewart Limited, 1966), p. 7.
2. John H. Land, "Record of Robert Land, U.E.L.," *Papers and Records of the Wentworth Historical Society*, vol. 7 (Hamilton: Spectator Printing Co., 1892-1924) p. 5.
3. Nicholas Leblovic, "The Life and History of Richard Beasley, Esquire," The Bailey Memorial Lecture, 22 October 1965.
4. "The Gage Family," *The Wentworth Historical Society*, vol. 9 (Hamilton: Spectator Printing Co., 1892-1924) p. 15
5. These were passenger pigeons. Several descriptions of the day record so many pigeons in Eastern Canada that they blackened the sky. Settlers found that they were a good source of food, and hunted them into extinction. By the early 1900s, they had disappeared completely.
6. Quoted in T. Roy Woodhouse, "The Beginnings of the History of Hamilton" (an address to the Wentworth Historical Society, 10 April 1959).
7. J. Ross Robertson, ed., *The Diary of Mrs. John Graves Simcoe* (Toronto: W. Briggs, 1911), pp. 320-324.
8. Campbell, *A Mountain*, p. 40.
9. Woodhouse, "The Beginnings," p. 25.

Chapter 2
1. Because the subdivision documents are undated, it is not known if Hamilton subdivided his property prior to it being designated the judicial centre for the District of Gore or afterwards.
2. *City of Hamilton 1884, Hamilton and its Industries*, FILM CIHM 11067.
3. Marjorie Freeman Campbell, *A Mountain and a City* (Toronto: McClelland & Stewart Limited, 1966) p. 57
4. *City of Hamilton 1884*.
5. Quoted in Margaret Houghton, "North End," unpublished manuscript.
6. Charles A. Carter and Thomas M. Bailey, *The Diary of Sophia MacNab* (Hamilton: W.L. Griffon Ltd., 1968).
7. "George Rolph," *Dictionary of Hamilton Biography*, vol. 1 (Hamilton: W.L. Griffin Ltd., 1981) p. 172.
8. John Glasgow, "Fifty-Seven Years' Experience of Canadian Life," *The Wentworth Historical Society*, vol. 1 (Hamilton, Ont.: Spectator Printing Co., 1892).
9. Marjorie Freeman Campbell, *A Mountain and a City* (Toronto: McClelland & Stewart Ltd., 1966), p. 66.
10. *History of the Fire Department of Hamilton, 1920*, FILM CIHM 73974.
11. "Peter Desjardins," *The Wentworth Historical Society*, #26 (Hamilton: Spectator Printing Co., 1892-1924).
12. Ibid.
13 *The Spectator*, 2 January 1897.
14. D.R. Beer, "Sir Allan Napier MacNab," *Dictionary of Hamilton Biography*, vol. 1 (Hamilton: W.L. Griffin Ltd., 1981) 137.
15. *City of Hamilton 1884*.

Chapter 3
1. Quoted by J.H. Smith, "The City of Hamilton," *Papers and Records of the Wentworth Historical Society*, vol. 6 (Hamilton: Spectator Printing Co., 1892-1924) pp. 68-69.
2. Normal Helm, *In the Shadow of Giants: The Story of the Toronto, Hamilton and Buffalo Railway* (Cheltenham, Ont.: The Boston Mills Press, 1978).
3. Margaret McBurney and Mary Byers, *Tavern in the Town: Early Inns and Taverns of Ontario* (Toronto: University of Toronto Press, 1987).
4. James Elliott, "Passage from the Past," *The Spectator*, 16 March 1996.
5. Ibid.
6. Ibid.
7. *The Central School Jubilee Reunion*, August 1903, FILM CIHM 73356.
8. "Former Coloured Colony on Mount," *The Spectator*, 15 July 1936.
9. Elliott, "Passage from the Past."
10. Michael Quigley, "Cantatas, Cadenzas and Conductors," *The Head of the Lake Historical Society*, vol. 14 (Hamilton: Eagle Press, 1984).

11. "Burlington Ladies Academy of Hamilton," *Canada West*, 1847, FILM CIHM 55448.
12. Michael B. Katz, *The People of Hamilton, Canada West* (Cambridge, Mass.: Harvard University Press, 1975), p. 187.
13. Gustaveus Myers, *A History of Canadian Wealth* (Toronto: James, Lewis and Samuel Publishers, 1972), p. 189.
14. Frankin Davey McDowell, "One Hundred Years of the Great Western Railway" (an address to the Head of the Lake Historical Society, 2 October 1953).
15. Marjorie Freeman Campbell, *A Mountain and a City* (Toronto: McClelland & Stewart, 1966), p. 109.
16. *The Daily Spectator*, 13 March 1857.
17. Campbell, *A Mountain*, p. 112. Campbell calls the epidemic "cholera," but as Richard Moll has pointed out, it was typhoid fever brought in by impoverished Irish immigrants.
18. *The Spectator*, 1 January 1861.

Chapter 4
1. Isaac Buchanan, M.P., "Speech, 1863," FILM CIHM 51900.
2. C.M. Johnston, *The Head of the Lake: A History of Wentworth County* (Hamilton: Robert Duncan and Company Ltd., 1958), p. 240.
3. *The Spectator*, 2 July 1867.
4. Michael B. Katz, *The People of Hamilton, Canada West* (Cambridge, Mass.: Harvard University Press, 1975), p. 3.
5. Alex Wingfield, "The Nine Hour Pioneers," quoted in Bryan D. Palmer, *A Culture in Conflict* (Montreal: McGill-Queen's University Press, 1979), p. 142.
6. Greg Kealey, *Canada Investigates Industrialism* (Toronto: University of Toronto Press, 1973), p. 145.
7. Hamilton Public Library, Hamilton Collection, *Recollections of John Peebles, Mayor of Hamilton, 1930-1933*, February 1946.
8. *History of the Fire Department of Hamilton, 1920*, FILM CIHM 73974.
9. John B. Buckingham, *A Short History of the Ancient Order of Foresters, Hamilton, Ontario*, FILM CIHM 15620.
10. Palmer, *A Culture*, p. 52.
11. "The Spectator, Carnival Edition," August 1889, FILM CIHM 38550.
12. Thomas E. Champion, *The 13th Battalion of Hamilton, 1897*, FILM CIHM 14666.
13. Ibid.
14. Ibid.
15. *The Spectator*, 8 April 1878.
16. *The Spectator*, Carnival Edition, August 1889.

Chapter 5
1. Donald Avery, *Dangerous Foreigners* (Toronto: McClelland & Stewart Ltd., 1979), pp. 8-9.
2. For a good discussion of these issues and Hamilton workers' reactions to them, see Bryan D. Palmer, *A Culture in Conflict* (Montreal: McGill-Queen's University Press, 1979).
3. Hamilton Public Library, Special Collections, *Hamilton Street Railway Strike*, www.hpl.hamilton.on.ca/local/spcoll/strike.htm.
4. Ibid., p. 166.
5. Brian Henley, "Adelaide Hoodless Blazed a Trail," *The Spectator*, 6 March 1993.
6. *The Spectator*, 12 July 1975.
7. Wayne Roberts, ed., *Organizing Westinghouse: Alf Ready's Story* (Hamilton: McMaster University, Labour Studies Programme), Publication 79-01.
8. Quoted in C.M. Johnston, *The Head of the Lake: A History of Wentworth County* (Hamilton: Robert Duncan & Company, Ltd., 1958), p. 245.
9. Hamilton Public Library, Special Collections, *Hamilton Radials*, p. 27.
10. J. Brian Henley, "Moving Pictures Cause Uproar," *The Spectator*, 1 June 1985.

Chapter 6
1. *The Spectator*, 7 June 1939.
2. Carolyn Gray, "Marion Stinson (Crerar)," *Dictionary of Hamilton Biography*, Vol. II (Hamilton: W.L. Griffin Ltd., 1991) pp. 156-159.

3. *The Spectator*, 7 January 1921.
4. *The Spectator*, 15 April 1921.
5. These and many other advertisements for women workers are listed in the pages of the January 1920 issues of *The Spectator*.
6. *The Spectator*, 27 May 1920.
7. P.M., "Elizabeth Bagshaw," *Dictionary of Hamilton Biography*, Vol. IV (Hamilton: Seldon, Griffin Graphics, 1999) pp. 16-18.
8. James Dubro and Robin F. Rowland, *King of the Mob: Rocco Perri and the Woman Who Ran His Rackets* (Toronto: Penguin Books, 1987).
9. John Weaver, *Hamilton, An Illustrated History* (Toronto: James Lorimer and Company, Publishers, 1982), p. 141.
10. The covenants stated that lands could not be sold to Negroes, Asiatics, Bulgarians, Austrians, Russians, Serbs, Rumanians, Turks, Armenians, foreign-born Italians, Greeks, or Jews. Despite these restrictions, by the 1950s, a wide mix of people were living in Westdale.
11. Saskatchewan suffered more than any other Canadian province in the 1930s as a result of the collapse of commodity prices and the drought.
12. L.M. Grayson and Michael Bliss, eds., *The Wretched of Canada* (Toronto: University of Toronto Press, 1971), pp. 82-84.

Chapter 7
1. Quoted in "The Fortieth Anniversary... '46 Strike," *Special Steel Shots Supplement*, July 1986.
2. John Weaver, *Hamilton: An Illustrated History* (Toronto: James Lorimer and Company, Publishers, 1982), p. 137.
3. *The Spectator*, 10 July 1976.
4. Quoted in Bill Freeman, *1005: Political Life in a Union Local* (Toronto: James Lorimer and Company, Publishers, 1982), p. 56.
5. *The Spectator*, 22 July 1946.
6. *The Spectator*, 2 August 1946.
7. Weaver, *Hamilton*, pp. 162-169.
8. *The Spectator*, 7 June 1954.
9. Thanks to James Elliott of *The Spectator* for first writing about John Holland.

Chapter 8
1. Marjorie Freeman Campbell, *A Mountain and a City* (Toronto: McClelland & Stewart Ltd., 1966), p. 270.
2. I have written about Hamilton's urban renewal projects in more detail in Bill Freeman and Marsha Hewitt, *Their Town: The Mafia, the Media and the Party Machine* (Toronto: James Lorimer and Company, Publishers, 1979).
3. *The Spectator*, 10 April 1965.
4. *The Spectator*, 21 July 1978.
5. *The Toronto Star*, 24 January 2000, p. C3.
6. *The Spectator*, 19 June 1972.
7. *The Spectator*, 16 December 1999.
8. The Ontario Workers' Arts and Heritage 1930s interview project often spilled over into later decades. Musician Fred Puser was close friends with the Washington family of musicians who were very well known in Hamilton music circles.
9. Emily Friedman and Ariel Rogers, "Stan Rogers: A Short Biography," from CD liner notes for *Home in Halifax*.
10. For a description of Papalia's career, see Adrian Humphreys, *The Enforcer, Johnny Pops Papalia, A Life and Death in the Mafia* (Toronto: Harper Collins, 1999).

Chapter 9
1. *The Globe and Mail*, 12 March 2001.
2. *Hamilton's Newest Facts and Figures* (Hamilton: Community Planning and Development Division, May 1999), p. 13.
3. *The Spectator*, 15 August 1995.
4. *Hamilton's Newest Facts*, p. 1.
5. *Where the Rubber Hits the Road* (Red Canoe Productions, January 2001).
6. Thanks to Brian Henly for first retelling this story. *The Spectator*, 15 June 1996.